The Ark Of The COVENANT

And Other Secret Weapons Of The Ancients

THE ARK OF THE COVENANT
AND OTHER SECRET WEAPONS OF THE ANCIENTS

by
David Medina
With Additional Material By Timothy Green Beckley, Sean Casteel, Olav Phillips, Brad Steiger and Tim Swartz

This edition Copyright 2014 by Timothy Green Beckley

Published in the United States of America By
Timothy Green Beckley
Box 753 · New Brunswick, NJ 08903

Staff Members
Timothy G. Beckley, Publisher
Carol Ann Rodriguez, Assistant to the Publisher
Sean Casteel, General Associate Editor
Tim R. Swartz, Graphics and Editorial Consultant
William Kern, Typesetting, Formatting & Cover Design

Sign Up On The Web For Our Free Weekly Newsletter
and Mail Order Version of Conspiracy Journal and Bizarre Bazaar
www.ConspiracyJournal.com

Order Hot Line: 1-732-602-3407
PayPal: MrUFO8@hotmail.com

TABLE OF CONTENTS

INTRODUCTION

AN OBJECT OF WONDERMENT

By Timothy Green Beckley

The Ark of the Covenant has always been an object of great wonderment. Biblical scholars have debated its uses for years, while the public fantasizes about its powers. Moviemakers have attempted to tell the story of this gleaming gold artifact in epic fictionalized form.

Made to be a receptacle in which the Ten Commandments given Moses could be safeguarded, the Ark also had the power to destroy the enemies of the Israelites.

I met David Medina while in the UK to speak before the House of Lords UFO group. He presented me with his privately printed manuscript on the Ark and told me he would like to see it get wider distribution. I put out a limited edition of his manuscript and I found that people were intrigued by the subject. They wanted to learn all they could about the Ark. Was there really enough evidence to prove that it had actually existed? Did God create this device for the purposes stated? And above all else, what gave the Ark its immense power? And, of course, we would like to know if the Ark still exists to this day – and, if so, WHERE?

We believe David's work is the most accurate on the subject. It gets right to the heart of the matter and reveals knowledge heretofore kept secret. However, we wanted readers to take the complete "tour" of the weapons of mass destruction from the ancient world and have thus supplemented Mr. Medina'sextensive coverage of the Ark, its creation and purposes, with material on other weapons of antiquity, including the possible existence of ancient nuclear weapons, magical swords and other tools of destruction. Could it have been that the gods were in reality extraterrestrials who traveled to this planet on a regular basis?

Tim Beckley mrufo8@hotmail.com

Tim Beckley approaches a replica of the Ark of the Covenant
very carefully, so as not to awaken a sleeping giant.

Photo by Lady Suzanne Miller

THE ARK OF THE COVENANT
PREFACE

Until I saw the film, "Chariots of the Gods," I knew very little about the Ark of the Covenant. In the film it was mentioned that two students in the United States had made a replica and that it gave off such a high electric charge that they were ordered to destroy it. Yet, in the book by the same title, Erich von Daniken does not claim that a replica was actually made and I have been able to find no evidence that it was. However, my interest was aroused and, when a friend gave me a Bible as a birthday gift, I extracted every detail I could find about the ark, compared my Bible with other versions, and began searching for anything written on the subject. To my surprise, I found very little accurate information. Once I had started, I knew that I had to continue trying to find what the ark really was and how it functioned.

Fortunately, I met a radiographer who was also interested in the subject. In addition to explaining a lot, she lent me a book on electromagnetism. Although I did not understand the text, I could see from the diagrams that when solenoids are arranged in certain alignments, they will intensify and direct electric currents. I was now faced with a problem: my lack of technical knowledge prevented me from proving that what I postulated was possible.

I decided to prepare a manuscript and circulate copies amongst those with requisite knowledge to answer the questions which I posed. After a year, I was still trying to find a scientist who would answer even one question. Seemingly, the only way was to publish the monograph with the questions unanswered. Then no doubt the experts who read it would either acclaim or debunk it.

Several publishers praised the manuscript but for one reason or another felt it would not be a profitable undertaking. I knew that they were probably right, and so I decided to undertake the project myself, and thus the British edition came into being. This, I should remind you, was way before the movie "Raiders of the Lost Ark" was released.

This book is divided into two parts. The first tells how Moses received the instructions for building the Ark of the Covenant and describes in detail how every article was made. The detail is important and is set out in such a way that the reader can easily refer back whilst following the progress of the ark during the four-hundred and fifty years of its existence in the second part. It is deliberately devoid of spiritual interpretation but adequate references are included to enable readers to look up the appropriate text and form their own conclusions.

The history of the ark indicates that it was a powerful electrical generator and possibly a nuclear reactor. Also, the possibility that it was a two-way radio, capable of reaching the outer limits of space, cannot be overlooked. Bible students ponder over the construction of the tabernacle and its furnishings, for although precise instructions and exact measurements are quoted, some aspects contain insufficient details to enable the whole to be reconstructed. No mention is made of the electrical components, and somehow, harmless ornamental borders, etcetera, have been substituted for them.

For centuries, it was thought that the first five books of the Bible, namely: Genesis, Exodus, Leviticus, Numbers and Deuteronomy, were written by Moses. However, it is now known that there were at least four authors. It is also known that the Levites, who were the high priests, changed some of the laws contained in the book of Leviticus to suit the times. Whilst the ark existed, the Levites were responsible for it, though only a few of them were aware of the full secrets of its power. Probably these clever and inspired men wisely re-described some of the components to obscure the obvious truth yet left enough evidence for the diligent enquirers to reconstruct the original meaning at a future date when the time was right for it to be known.

I know that other people in various parts of the world are conducting research in the mysteries of the Ark of the Covenant, but I know of no other book which relates the whole story. The only other texts that I have read are those to which I refer.

Despite the expense involved in researching this subject, I have no regrets in pursuing the project, which has brought me into contact with so many interesting people and publications. My research has marked the start of an adventure coupled with the excitement of discovery.

At the time that I was preparing my manuscript for publication, two engineers, George Sassoon and Rodney Dale, were also researching the Ark of the Covenant. By translating the original text of the Kabbalah (called the Zohar), they discovered that the manna, which sustained the Israelites in the wilderness for forty years, was produced by a machine. Their article, "Deus est machina?" (New Scientist), was followed by two books, "The Manna Machine" and "The Kabbalah Decoded." They claim that the Ark of the Covenant in the Bible is the same as the manna-machine (Ancient of Days) in the Kabbalah. However, my belief is that the two pieces of equipment coexisted, and that the ark provided the power for the manna producing machine.

Like the work of Sassoon and Dale which prompted Erich von Daniken to write "Signs of the Gods?" (with the first chapter entitled, "In Search of the Ark of the Covenant"), I believe that my small effort helped to arouse the interest of other authors and resulted in some recently published articles. Prior to 1977, very little accurate information about the ark had been published.

The exciting film, "Raiders of the Lost Ark," though a product of fiction-fantasy, is based on the idea that the Ark of the Covenant once existed and may one day be discovered. As yet, I have not received any scientific appraisal of my writing, even though there are rumors that replicas of the ark have been produced in France and Belgium. However, a few readers have shared their own discoveries with me and some are contained in the text of this edition.

My thanks are extended to: Janet Calow, Betty Collins, Anne Dinsdale, Ann Griffin, and Rev. Douglas Webster, all of whom have assisted in various ways.

David Medina

Throughout the text of this book various abbreviations are used. They are as follows:

ABBREVIATIONS

AV The Authorized Version of the Apocrypha.

JB The Jerusalem Bible.

KJV The King James Version of the Holy Bible.

NEB The New English Bible.

OT Old Testament.

RSV The Revised Standard Version of the Holy Bible.

RV The Revised Version of the Apocrypha.

THE ARK OF THE COVENANT AND OTHER SECRET WEAPONS OF THE ANCIENTS

PART ONE

After receiving the Ten Commandments on Mount Sinai, Moses was given full instructions for the building of the container into which the two tablets of stone were to be placed. A vessel or hollow receptacle used for conveyance was called an ark. The commandments were known as the covenant (or testimony).

The Ark of the Covenant was housed in a huge tent or tabernacle which was the Israelites' temple during the forty years which they spent wandering in the wilderness. The tabernacle also contained an incense altar, a small table, and a large, seven-pronged, candlestick or lamp stand. The sacrificial altar was outside the tabernacle and the whole area of the court or public space was fenced by curtains supported by metal posts.

THE TABERNACLE

The tent, or tabernacle, was draped over a framework in gold plated wood. Each frame was 2'3" wide and 15' high, and had twin tenons at the bottom which fitted into silver sockets. On the south side of the tabernacle there were twenty frames, and the same on the north side. Each of these two sides was therefore 45' long and 15' high. On the west side, or the back of the tabernacle, there were six frames, which indicate that the tabernacle was 13'6" wide. There were two further

THE ARK OF THE COVENANT AND OTHER SECRET WEAPONS OF THE ANCIENTS

frames for the corners at the back of the tabernacle. The purpose of the two additional frames has never been satisfactorily explained and the Bible versions vary:

KJV "And two boards shalt thou make for the corners of the tabernacle in the two sides.

"And they shall be coupled together beneath, and they shall be coupled together above the head of it unto one ring: thus it shall be for them both; they shall be for the two corners.

RSV "And you shall make two frames for the corners of the tabernacle in the rear; they shall be separate beneath, but joined at the top, at the first ring; thus it shall be for both of them; they shall form the two corners."

JB "You are to make two frames for the corners at the back of the tabernacle. These frames must be coupled at the lower end and so to the top, up to the level of the first ring; this for the two frames that are to form the two corners."

The frames were held together by fifteen gold plated, wooden bars, five for each side. (Some translators claim that there were only three bars on the west side.). Also, a middle bar ran from one end to the other, halfway up. The frames had gold rings on them to take the bars.

Moses was to erect the tabernacle in accordance with the model which he was shown on the mountain. Without this model, it is difficult to understand what part the bars played in the construction.

Some of the rings into which the bars fitted may have been holes, but what was the function of the middle bar which ran from end to end? It was halfway up – that is a height of 7'-6". To extend from the frames on the west side, to the entrance on the eastern extremity, it would have needed to be over 45' in length. What was it attached to on the east

THE ARK OF THE COVENANT AND OTHER SECRET WEAPONS OF THE ANCIENTS

side? One of the pillars which formed the entrance, perhaps.

THE CURTAINS

The tent was made with ten curtains of fine twined linen, in blue, purple and scarlet, with cherubim embroidered on them. Each curtain measured 42' x 61. Two sets of five curtains were sewn together forming two sheets measuring 42' x 30'. The two sheets were then joined by fifty gold clasps inserted in the loops of blue ribbon on the edge of each sheet.

When the two sheets were coupled together, the material measured 42' x 60'. The framework over which they were draped (refer Diagram 1) measured 45' x 13'6" x 15' high. This means that there would have been 9" of framework showing below the drapes on each side, unless, as is probable, they were hung inside the framework. As the framework was 451 long, and the material 601, there would be 716" of material left over at each end. The framework was 15'6" wide and the western side (or back) could be covered by the excess of 7'6" on the north and the south sides and the overlap from the top reaching halfway (7'6") down. We are not told how the edges were joined.

The linen tent was covered by another tent comprised of eleven curtains of goats' hair, each measured 451 x 6'. Five curtains were sewn together, and the other six sewn together. The two resultant sheets were then coupled together with fifty brass clasps which were passed through loops on the edge of each sheet.

KJV "... and shalt double the sixth curtain in the forefront of the tabernacle."

The extra six feet was used to form a double door.

KJV "And the remnant that remaineth of the curtains of the tent, the half curtain that remaineth, shall hang over the backside of the tabernacle."

THE ARK OF THE COVENANT AND OTHER SECRET WEAPONS OF THE ANCIENTS

NEB "The additional length of the tent hanging is to fall over the back of the Tabernacle."

The extra 7'-6" on the west side was to be folded over in the same way as the linen.

Because the goats' hair curtains were 3' longer than the linen curtains, they would have covered the sides completely, leaving 9" to spare at the bottom.

Above the goats' hair, there was a covering of rams' skins dyed red, and a further covering of badgers' skins above that. No sizes are given.

Presumably, the goats' hair was first spun into thread, and then woven. As the larger of the two sheets of goats' hair was towards the front of the tabernacle, the join made by the fifty brass clasps would be in the same position as the join made by the fifty gold clasps in the linen sheets.

The KJV and the RSV both state that the final covering was of badgers' skins. The Jerusalem Bible states leather, and the NEB porpoise hides. Also the NEB omits that the rams' skins were dyed red.

According to the KJV, the framework of the tent was comprised of "boards." The NEB states "planks." It is unlikely that the linen curtains were draped over the framework, for, had it been solid, the beautiful embroidery would not have been seen. They are more likely to have been hung inside the frames. Thus, the outside of the tabernacle would have been fully conductive and the inside completely insulated and electrically safe.

The purple dye used for coloring the curtains was obtained from the hypo-branichial glands of the gastropod mollusk (Murex brandaris and Murex tranculus). At that time, a purple industry flourished in the city of Tyre.

THE ARK OF THE COVENANT AND OTHER SECRET WEAPONS OF THE ANCIENTS

KJV "And thou shalt rear up the tabernacle according to the fashion thereof which was shewed thee in the mount."

THE VEIL

The veil, which hung inside the tent to divide the "holy" place from the "most holy," was made from fine linen, colored blue, purple and scarlet, and embroidered with cherubim. The four pillars, from which it hung, were made of wood and overlaid with gold. No sizes are mentioned. The pillars were mounted on four silver sockets, and the hooks to which the veil was fastened were made of gold.

The veil was hung under the gold clasps which joined the two sheets of linen and the brass clasps which joined the two sheets of goats' hair. Thus, the "holy" space and the "most holy" would each have measured 22'-6" x 13'-6".

THE DOOR

The hanging door of the tent was made from linen, colored blue, purple and scarlet. These drapes were embroidered, but the motif is not mentioned. The five pillars, from which the door hung, were made of wood and overlaid with gold. The hooks were made of gold, and the pillars fitted into brass sockets.

The middle bar, which extended from one end of the frames to the other, halfway up, may have been fastened to the center pillar in the entrance. In this case, the veil was either not in one piece, or there was a hole exactly in the center of it to allow the bar to pass through.

How the five pillars at the entrance to the tent were arranged is not stated. The drapes were presumably hung at the end of the framework. Above, and on each side of the door, there would have been 7'-6" of the linen (inner) tent, and 13'-6" of the goats' hair tent. The Jerusalem Bible suggests that an awning was formed with the goats' hair material.

THE ARK OF THE COVENANT AND OTHER SECRET WEAPONS OF THE ANCIENTS

THE CONTENTS OF THE TABERNACLE

In the "most holy" space, behind the veil, was placed the ark (or box) which contained the two tablets of stone on which the commandments (or covenant, or testimony) were written. The mercy seat was placed upon the ark. In the "holy" space, outside the veil, the incense altar was placed in front of the ark, a small table was placed on the north side of the tent, and a large seven pronged candlestick on the south side.

OUTSIDE THE TABERNACLE

The sacrificial altar was placed outside the doorway of the tent. Also a laver (or washstand) was placed in the doorway.

THE COURT

The court (or public space) was 150' long on the south and the north sides. This was comprised of fine twined linen hung from twenty silver pillars on each side. The west side was 75' wide with ten pillars. The gate was on the east side.

On each side of the gate, there was 22'-6" of hanging linen supported by three posts. The gate was 30' wide and the hangings were of blue, purple, scarlet and fine twined linen, wrought with needle work. The gate was supported by four pillars. The fillets and hooks of all the pillars were of silver and the sockets of brass. All of the pins (or tent-pegs) and the vessels for use in the tabernacle were made of brass. The height of the court was 7'-6" (Refer Diagram 3.)

THE ARK AND THE MERCY SEAT

The ark was a wooden box, 3'-9" long, 2'-3" broad, and 2'-3" high. It was overlaid with pure gold, both inside and outside, and had a "crown of gold" round the top edge. In each corner there was a gold ring into which the staves for carrying the ark were fitted. As the staves were not to be removed, it is probable that they were fixed to the rings.

THE ARK OF THE COVENANT AND OTHER SECRET WEAPONS OF THE ANCIENTS

The lid of the ark was called a mercy seat and was made of pure gold, 3'-9" long and 2'-3" broad. At each end there was a cherub, looking toward the other across the seat, with their wings spread high, so that they covered the mercy seat. (A cherub was not a plump naked, winged infant, but a winged lion with a human head.)

According to the instructions given to Moses, God would speak to him from above the mercy seat, between the two cherubim. The cherubim were beaten out of one piece of gold. They were probably hollow, for had they been solid, the mercy seat would have been too heavy to move.

The electric currents may have started from a chemical reaction which occurred where the two tablets of stone came into contact with the gold plates. The two gold cherubim may have acted as positive and negative poles so that an arc occurred between them. The Bible clearly states that both the interior and the exterior of the ark were covered with gold.

However, had the top edge of the ark (or box) been left bare, the wood would have insulated one surface from the other.

Why were there two tablets of stone? Positive and negative magnetism?

The wooden, gold-covered staves by which the ark was carried were placed in the gold rings at the four corners of the ark. As they were not to be removed, they may have acted as legs when the ark was stationary; thus the ark would have been both elevated and earthed. Probably, the "crown of gold" was a coil, which acted as a solenoid.

THE INCENSE ALTAR

The wooden, gold covered incense altar measured 1'-6" x 1'-6" x 3' high.

KJV "And he made the incense altar of shittim wood: the length of

THE ARK OF THE COVENANT AND OTHER SECRET WEAPONS OF THE ANCIENTS

it-was a cubit, and the breadth of it was cubit; it was foursquare and two cubits was the height of it; and the horns thereof were of the same."

KJV "And he overlaid it with pure gold, both the top of it, and the sides thereof round about, and the horns of it; also he made unto it a crown of gold round about."

Gold rings were attached to two of the corners under the crown or solenoid, so that it could be carried with the wooden, gold covered staves.

Interpreters are puzzled by the "horns" and tend to think that the "crown of gold" was merely an ornamental border. Animal horns can have some use in the transmission of electricity. Both the crown on the incense altar and the one on the ark could have been coils which acted as solenoids.

THE TABLE

The table was 3' x 1'-6" x 2'-3" high.

KJV "And thou shall overlay it with pure gold, and make thereto a crown of gold round about.

KJV "And thou shalt make unto it a border of a hand breadth round about, and thou shalt make a golden crown to the border thereof round about.

KJV "And thou shalt make for it four rings of gold, and put the rings in the four corners that are on the feet thereof.

"Over against the border shall the rings be for places of the staves to bear the table."

The staves for carrying the table were made from gold-covered wood. The spoons and dishes, etc., to be used on the table, were made of pure gold.

The table was to be set with shewbread at all times.

According to the wording of the KJV (which differs from the RSV), there was a crown of gold round the top of the table and another on the border round the bottom of the legs. The RSV states that there was but one "moulding" of gold. The NEB calls the crowns of gold "bands" and the border on the table a "rim." However, the description of the crowns on the table differs from those on the ark and the incense altar: a border is added. The RSV suggests that the border was just a "frame" to hold the ornamental "moulding." The Bible does not state from what material the border was made, and it may have been an iron core for the solenoid, or perhaps an insulator. There were no "horns" on the table.

THE CANDLESTICK

The candlestick was beaten out of pure gold.

From the stem there protruded three branches on each side. These were curved upwards, so that their tops were the same level as the stem. The bowls were the shape of almonds and there were three in each of the six branches. In the stem there were four bowls. All the bowls were decorated with a knop (or bud) and a flower. The seven lamps together with the tongs and the snuff dishes were made of pure gold. The only guide given to the size of the candlestick is that one talent of gold was used. Moses was told to do the work in exactly the way he was shown on the mount.

The candlestick could perhaps be better described as a lamp stand. Seemingly, it stood on the ground and would have been the same height as the small table (2-3"). The shape of the candlestick suggests that it was an antenna.

THE LAVER

Unlike the contents of the tabernacle, the laver (or washbasin) was made of brass from the mirrors collected from the women. It had a short pedestal with a wide base, but no sizes are mentioned. Water was placed in the laver for Aaron (the high priest) and his sons (who were also priests) to wash their hands and feet, "that they die not . . ."

The water-filled, brass laver was yet another instrument by which the power of the ark could be transmitted to the sacrificial altar outside the tabernacle, and beyond. As it was made from brass which had previously been used as mirrors, it must have been a good reflector.

THE SACRIFICIAL ALTAR

The framework of the Sacrificial Altar was made from wood and covered with brass. It measured 7'-6" x 7'-6" x 4'-6" high. In the four corners there were horns, and these were overlaid with brass. All of the vessels and implements were made of brass. A brass mesh net was hung inside the frame from four brass rings looped over the horns. Wooden, brass-covered staves were used to carry the altar, and these fitted into brass rings on the two sides of it. The staves could also have been used to lift the grate from the frame.

This altar, like the incense altar, had horns on the corners. There was no "crown of gold" to act as a solenoid, but what part did the hanging, brass mesh grate play?

THE INCENSE

Only incense of the type contained in the instructions received by Moses were to be burnt on the incense altar. The gas would have contributed to the conduction of the electricity which emitted from the ark. Also a variety of spices were mixed to anoint the ark and all the other metal. These spices were: pure myrrh, sweet cinnamon, sweet calamus, cassia, olive oil, and hin.

This brew was not to be put upon a person's skin, and nobody else was to use the same formula. It was dangerous. Probably acid, which would definitely have made the ark an electric cell, for when acid comes into contact with gold and copper, electricity is produced.

THE PRIESTS CLOTHING

Aaron, the high priest, brother of Moses, was required to wear special clothing when ministering before the ark. Bible dictionaries are at variance regarding the description of the ephod. Usually, it was like a short, square- necked, sleeveless shirt. Aaron's was made with gold, purple, scarlet, blue, and fine twined linen, and it was embroidered. It had two shoulder pieces, joined at the two edges, and a girdle made from the same materials. On each shoulder of the ephod was an onyx stone set in gold.

The breastplate of judgment was made from the same materials as the ephod. It was 9" x 9" and the cloth was doubled. Twelve jewels were set into the breastplate. The Interpreters Bible Dictionary discredits the translations of the names of the stones, but according to the KJV they were:

SARDIUS

EMERALD

LIGURE

BERYL

TOPAZ

SAPPHIRE

AGATE

ONYX

CARBUNCLE

DIAMOND

THE ARK OF THE COVENANT AND OTHER SECRET WEAPONS OF THE ANCIENTS

AMETHYST

JASPER

The RSV replaces the ligure with a jacinth and the NEB states:

SARDIN

PURPLE GARNET

TURQUOISE

TOPAZ

CHRYSOLITE

LAPIS LAZULI

AGATE

CORNELIAN

GREEN FELDSPAR

JADE

JASPER

GREEN JASPER

The gold rings in the bottom corners of the breastplate were tied, with blue laces, to corresponding rings on the ephod. Golden chains were attached to the gold rings in the top corners of the breastplate, the other ends of the chain being attached to the setting of the onyx stones on the shoulders.

The robe of the ephod was blue. Pomegranates of blue, purple, and scarlet were attached to the hem of the robe, with golden bells between them.

KJV "And it shall be upon Aaron to minister; and his sound shall be heard when he goeth in unto the holy place before the Lord, and

THE ARK OF THE COVENANT AND OTHER SECRET WEAPONS OF THE ANCIENTS

when he cometh out, that he die not."

Aaron wore a miter on his head. The miters worn by the high priests usually consisted of a turban. Sometimes a piece of cloth was left hanging over the nape of the neck, and this could also be used as a veil for the face. A gold plate covered Aaron's forehead and was attached to the miter with blue laces. The outfit was completed by the addition of an embroidered coat of fine linen, a girdle of needle work, and linen underpants.

The four sons of Aaron were required to wear coats with girdles, bonnets, and linen underpants. The difference between a bonnet and a miter is not clear; the bonnet may have been a hood or cowl.

KJV "And they shall be upon Aaron, and upon his sons, when they come in unto the tabernacle of the congregation, or when they come near unto the altar to minister in the holy place, that they bear not iniquity and die . . ."

Only Aaron was permitted to enter the inner sanctum containing the ark, but his sons were presumably to stand by, ready to pull him out should his bells cease ringing, "that he die not." The gold plate on the front of the miter would have formed an eye shield and he was probably able to veil his face. Gold wire was woven into the blue, purple, and scarlet of the ephod. Apart from the protection offered by the gold and the colored linen, there were also the twelve jewels in the breastplate of judgment. The stones seemingly embraced all the colors of the spectrum and probably absorbed or repelled the radiation from the ark.

KJV "And thou shall put in the breastplate of judgment the Urim and the Thummim; and they shall be upon Aaron's heart, when he goeth before the Lord."

Until fairly recently, the Urim and Thummim were thought to be scrolls on which prayers were written. They are now believed to have

THE ARK OF THE COVENANT AND OTHER SECRET WEAPONS OF THE ANCIENTS

been two disks the size of draughts (or checkers). One side of each disk was white and the other black. After asking God a question, the priest withdrew the disks from their concealment. When both white sides were uppermost, the answer was "Yes!" Two black sides indicated "No!" When one was white and the other black, God had not yet made up his mind.

The above text is stripped of spiritual embroidery – and was not obtained from Amulets and Talismans – but the following extract is reproduced by permission of the Masters and Fellows of University College, Oxford, and Christ's College, Cambridge:

The disks were placed between the two layers of cloth from which the breastplate was made and could therefore be moved about behind the twelve jewels. Nobody knows how the disks were made or what they were made from. As we will see later in the story, something protected Aaron from the radiation of the ark and the breastplate of judgment may well have been a remote control panel.

SETTING UP THE TABERNACLE

On the first day of the first month in the second year after The Israelites were released from Egypt, the tabernacle was reared up at the base of Mount Sinai (also called Mount Horeb). Moses fastened the sockets, set up the framework, put the bars in place, and reared up the pillars. He then draped the linen and the goats' hair tents.

After placing the two tablets of stone in the ark, and putting the carrying poles in the rings, he placed the mercy seat on top of the ark. It was then carried into the back of the tabernacle. The veil, which divided the tabernacle in two, separating the "most holy" and the "holy" spaces, was then set up. (The ark was in the "most holy" space.)

The table was placed on north side of the "holy" space and set with bread. The candlestick was placed on the south side, and the seven lamps were lit.

THE ARK OF THE COVENANT AND OTHER SECRET WEAPONS OF THE ANCIENTS

The incense altar was positioned in front of the ark but was separated from it by the veil. The incense was set burning, and the hanging door of the tabernacle was set up.

The sacrificial altar was placed outside the hanging door, and the laver of water was put between it and the door.

The court (which measured 150' x 7' high) was then set up together with the hanging gate.

THE CLOUD

Whilst there was a cloud over the tabernacle, the Israelites remained camped, but when the cloud lifted they moved on. At night the cloud was replaced by a fiery glow.

THE ARK OF THE COVENANT AND OTHER SECRET WEAPONS OF THE ANCIENTS

PART TWO

THE HISTORY OF THE ARK

The first mention of the power of the ark is the eighth day after the consecration of Aaron, the brother of Moses, as high priest:

KJV "And Moses and Aaron went into the tabernacle of the congregation, and came out, and blessed the people; and the glory of the Lord appeared unto all the people.

"And there came a fire out from the Lord, and consumed upon the altar the burnt offering and the fat."

From the wording in the Bible it appears that Aaron burnt three separate offerings on the altar before "there came a fire out from the Lord." The writer meant to convey that the offerings were eventually burnt. The flesh and the hide of the calf were burnt outside the camp. It is unlikely that the fat and the kidneys of the calf were burnt on the altar, and then the rest of the animal carried outside the camp (a considerable distance) to be burnt; for that would have meant that the priests, and presumably the congregation, would then have had to retrace their steps back to the altar. Therefore, assuming that all three of the offerings were burnt at the same time, there would have been in the grate of

THE ARK OF THE COVENANT AND OTHER SECRET WEAPONS OF THE ANCIENTS

the altar: the fat and the kidneys of a young calf, a ram, and a young bullock; also the rump of a ram and a young bullock; and the dismembered carcasses of a ram, a young calf, a lamb, and a goat; as well as oiled bread. At this stage, Moses and Aaron went into the tabernacle of the congregation, out of sight, and came out again. What did they do whilst they were inside? Did they perhaps adjust the drapes so that the glory of the Lord would appear as Moses had told the people?

THE ARK OF THE COVENANT AND OTHER SECRET WEAPONS OF THE ANCIENTS

Apart from a laver in the doorway of the tabernacle of the congregation, the altar was the only item of brass in front of the ark. Had there been only air in the tabernacle, a thirty megavolt charge would have been necessary for electricity to span the gap between the two cherubim on the mercy seat and the brass mesh basket of the sacrificial altar and ignite the fat and oil. However, the tent was full of smoke from the incense altar in front of the ark and the air would have been ionized. Also, the other items in the tabernacle would have assisted the conduction.

Contrary to the instructions received by Moses, two of Aaron's sons, Nadab and Abihu, took up censers.

KJV "And there went a fire out from the Lord, and devoured them, and they died before the Lord."

The Lord was between the cherubim on the mercy seat, and the censers were made of brass. The word "devoured" suggests that nothing remained of the two young priests, but this was not so. Their bodies were carried outside the camp in their coats. Moses then warned Aaron, and his two remaining sons, Eleazar and Ithamar, not to uncover their heads or tear their clothing (which was the usual sign of mourning) "lest ye die."

According to Immanuel Velikovsky in "Worlds in Collision," the heat from the censers, carried by Nadab and Abihu, ignited deposits of Naphtha (or crude petroleum) which had fallen from a passing comet and seeped into cracks in the ground. However, the two men died instantly. They could not have burnt to death, for their clothing was still intact when they were carried from the camp. Also the heat from the huge fire on the altar would have been far greater than that which the censers produced.

After the death of his two nephews, Moses was told to warn Aaron not to come into the "most holy" place, within the veil before the mercy

THE ARK OF THE COVENANT AND OTHER SECRET WEAPONS OF THE ANCIENTS

seat, too often, "that he die not." Once again, he was warned to wash himself and to put on the protective clothing. After detailed instructions regarding offerings to be made, Aaron is told to go inside the veil with a censer and to burn incense on the incense altar and allow the smoke to cover the mercy seat, "that he die not." Previously, it was stated that the Lord would appear as a cloud upon the mercy seat.

Although it was dangerous to hold a censer anywhere near the ark, Aaron was protected in some way. His clothing was far more elaborate than that of his sons. He also wore the jeweled breastplate containing the Urim and Thummim.

THE ARK OF THE COVENANT AND OTHER SECRET WEAPONS OF THE ANCIENTS

Before moving their camp at the base of Mount Sinai, the Israelites were numbered by Moses and Aaron. They counted a total of 603,550 men who were over 20 and able to fight. This did not include the Levites, for they were appointed custodians of the tabernacle and all the associated equipment. There were 22,000 Levite males over one month old.

Detailed instructions were given regarding the way in which each item was to be covered when carried away by the Kohath section of the Levites.

The ark was covered with the red rams' skins, badgers' skins, and a blue cloth. The other items of gold were either covered by, or wrapped in, blue cloth and badgers' skins. The small table for the shewbread had an additional covering of purple cloth. The brass utensils associated with the altar were placed in the brass mesh grate, under the badgers' skins which covered the (brass) altar. The ashes from the altar were taken away and covered with purple cloth. Only when everything had been covered were the Kohaths permitted to come near. They were warned to touch nothing holy, "lest they die."

It may be said that the warning to the Kohaths was intended to deter them from stealing the golden vessels, for which the punishment would have been death. However, they were not permitted near until Aaron and his two sons, wearing their protective clothing, had covered (or insulated) them.

KJV "But thus do unto them, that they may live, and not die, when they approach the most holy things: Aaron and his sons shall go in, and appoint them every one to his service and to his burden.

KJV "But they shall not go in to see when the holy things are covered, lest they die."

The Gershonites were placed in charge of all the curtains, drapes, and coverings. The Merarites were responsible for the boards, pillars,

THE ARK OF THE COVENANT AND OTHER SECRET WEAPONS OF THE ANCIENTS

sockets, etc.

During the day, a cloud covered the tent which housed the ark, and at night, "the appearance of fire." Whilst the cloud covered the tent, the Israelites stayed where they were, but when the cloud lifted, they moved camp.

The cloud may have resulted from the vast quantity of incense which was continually burning. Some gases glow when electrical currents pass through them, as in neon signs. Moses would have known when it was best to strike camp and where to pitch it next.

Thirteen months after leaving Egypt, the camp moved from the wilderness of Sinai to the wilderness of Paran.

KJV "And when the people complained, it displeased the Lord; and the Lord heard it; and his anger was kindled; and the fire of the Lord burnt among them, and consumed them that were in the uttermost parts of the camp."

The Lord was on the mercy seat above the ark. Therefore, "the fire of the Lord" would have come from the mercy seat whilst camp was being set up in the new location, probably when the insulating covers were removed.

(Velikovsky claims that the fire resulted from the ignition of Naphtha in the cracks of the ground.)

The complaint of the people was that they had no meat, fish, vegetables, or fruit to eat. All that they had was manna. Moses was upset by all the bickering and told the people what the Lord had said to him: that they would eat flesh for a whole month, till it ran out of their noses.

The next day, a huge flock of quails was blown in from the sea, and they fell in heaps three feet high, in a circle round the camp at the radius of one day's journey. The people gathered up all the quails, but, as soon as they began to eat them, they fell sick and died. They called

THE ARK OF THE COVENANT AND OTHER SECRET WEAPONS OF THE ANCIENTS

the place Kibrothhattaavah, and after they had buried the dead they moved camp to Hazeroth.

Obviously, the small birds flew into the circumference of the radiation emitted by the ark and fell dead in a circle. Those who ate the birds died from radiation sickness. As soon as the dead were buried the camp was moved from the contaminated area.

KJV "And the manna was as coriander seed, and the color thereof as the color of bdellium.

THE ARK OF THE COVENANT AND OTHER SECRET WEAPONS OF THE ANCIENTS

KJV "And the people went about, and gathered it, and ground it in mills, or beat it in a mortar, and baked it in pans, and made cakes of it; and the taste of it was as the taste of fresh oil.

KJV "And when the dew fell upon the camp at night, the manna fell upon it."

An article called "Deus est machina?" by electronics consultant George Sassoon and biologist Rodney Dale was published in the New Scientist, 1st April 1976, and followed by two books, "The Manna-machine" and "The Kabbalah Decoded." The joint authors have found

THE ARK OF THE COVENANT AND OTHER SECRET WEAPONS OF THE ANCIENTS

a machine capable of making manna described in the text of the Kabbalah. They suggest that the machine was the Ark of the Covenant, but the drawings in their article bear little resemblance to the biblical description.

Therefore, I believe that the two pieces of equipment coexisted and that the ark provided the power for the manna machine.

At this point in the narration, it is necessary to refer back to an earlier episode involving quails and manna.

KJV "And they took their journey from Elim, and all the congregation of the children of Israel came unto the wilderness of Sin, which is between Elim and Sinai, on the fifteenth day of the second month after departing out of the land of Egypt."

Thus the time and the place are established. The people now complained about the lack of food.

KJV "And Moses said, 'This shall be, when the Lord shall give you in the evening flesh to eat, and in the morning bread to the full.'

KJV "And it came to pass, that at even the quails came up, and covered the camp; and in the morning dew lay round about the host.

KJV "And when the dew that lay was gone up, behold, upon the face of the wilderness there lay a small round thing, as small as the hoarfrost on the ground.

KJV "And when the children of Israel saw it, they said one to another, 'It is manna,' for they wist not what it was. And Moses said unto them, 'This is the bread which the Lord hath given you to eat.'

KJV "And Moses said, 'Let no man leave of it till the morning.'

KJV "Notwithstanding they hearkened not unto Moses; but some of them left it until the morning, and it bred worms, and stank; and Moses was wroth with them.

THE ARK OF THE COVENANT AND OTHER SECRET WEAPONS OF THE ANCIENTS

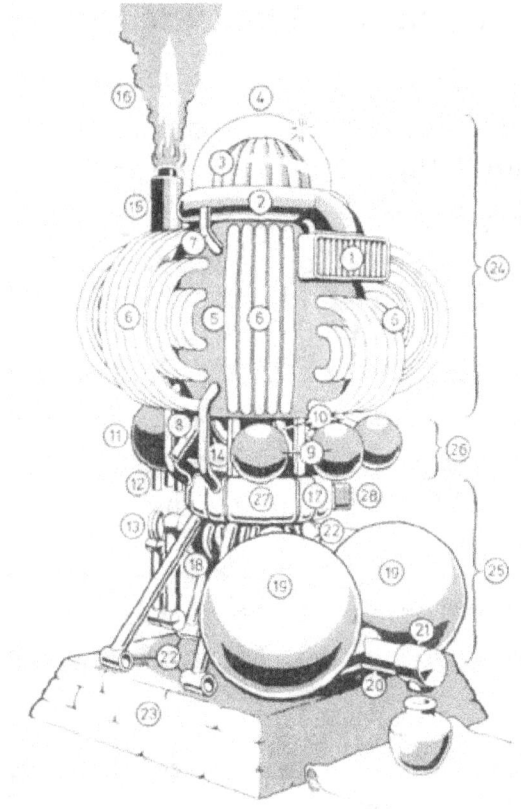

KJV "And they gathered it every morning, every man according to his eating; and when the sun waxed hot, it melted."

On this occasion, the quails were all over the vast camp and were alive. The people did not die or suffer any ill effects as a result of eating them. At this time, Moses had not received the commandments and the ark had not been built. However, "in the morning the dew lay round about the host."

What was the "host"? It may well have been the manna making machine. This raises the question of how the Israelites came into possession of such an intricate piece of equipment, but this is another subject and will not be dealt with here.

KJV "And it came to pass in the first month in the second year, on the first day of the month, that the tabernacle was reared up.

KJV "And he took and put the testimony into the ark, and set up the staves of the ark, and put the mercy seat above upon the ark;

KJV "And he brought the ark into the tabernacle, and set up the veil of the covering, and covered the ark of the testimony, as the Lord commanded Moses."

The two extra boards (or frames) at the corners of the tabernacle are a puzzle. They may have been set up in a different way from that shown in Diagram 1, and the excess of material in the curtains could have concealed the manna making machine.

THE ARK OF THE COVENANT AND OTHER SECRET WEAPONS OF THE ANCIENTS

The reader may be confused by the jumps in time. To reiterate:

Two and a half months after leaving Egypt, the Israelites reached the wilderness of Sin. They complained to Moses and Aaron about the lack of food. That evening a flock of quails flew into the camp and the people ate them. The next morning, they found manna on the ground. Almost two years later, the tabernacle was set up in the wilderness of Sinai.

Later, when the camp was in the wilderness of Paran, the people complained that they had only manna to eat. The next day, they found a heap of dead quails in a circle round the camp at radius one day's journey. Those who ate the birds became ill and died. The camp then moved to Hazeroth. The story resumes from there:

Aaron and his sister Miriam, the priestess, objected because Moses had married an Ethiopian woman. Together with Moses they went to the tabernacle:

KJV "And the cloud departed from off the tabernacle; and, behold Miriam became leprous, white as snow."

Miriam did not have leprosy, which is caused by bacteria and usually associated with poor living conditions. (The priests lacked little.) However, the radiation from the ark could have produced a skin condition which made Miriam appear leprous. Aaron (who would have been wearing his protective clothing) was very worried about his sister's condition. After being shut out of the camp for a week, Miriam was allowed to return, which indicates that she had recovered. After that experience, she would not dare to disagree with Moses again.

King Uzziah became leprous when he disagreed with the priests in the temple. (2 Chronicles 26.16-19)

The camp moved back to the wilderness of Paran.

Drastic action was required when Moses and Aaron found that

THE ARK OF THE COVENANT AND OTHER
SECRET WEAPONS OF THE ANCIENTS

they had a mutiny to deal with. The ringleader was Korah, who with the aid of Dathan, Abiram, and On, gathered together two hundred and fifty chiefs. These men were intelligent, well-known, and respected. The Lord had not spoken to them, and they doubted whether the Lord had said all that Moses claimed. Whether they were right or not, Moses was now forced either to defend his authority or lose it. So he told them to come to the tabernacle of the congregation the following day with their brass censers.

Two of the nephews of Moses were killed by fire when they took censers near the altar. (Leviticus 10.2)

The following morning, Korah gathered all the rebels outside the entrance to the tabernacle of the congregation.

Moses told the people to stand well clear of the tents of Korah, Dathan, and Abiram. (These men were Levites, and their tents would have been close to the tabernacle.) The three men came to the mouths of their respective tents, each with his wives and children.

Moses then told them that they would now see that what occurred was the work of the Lord and that he could not do it on his own.

He went on to say that if the three men died in the ordinary way it was not the work of the Lord. Whereas, if the ground opened under them, and they fell in, it would be the judgment of the Lord. (Moses did not say that he could not, or would not, cause this to occur.)

As soon as Moses had finished speaking, the ground under the three tents opened and everything fell into the fissures.

Those who were left were afraid and began to run away.

KJV "And there came a fire out from the Lord, and consumed the two hundred and fifty men that offered incense."

Aaron also carried a censer but was not killed.

THE ARK OF THE COVENANT AND OTHER SECRET WEAPONS OF THE ANCIENTS

Moses ordered the two-hundred and fifty censers to be gathered and made into broad plates to cover the altar. The passage ends with the warning that only the descendants of Aaron were to offer incense. Any others would suffer the same fate as the two-hundred and fifty.

The next day the people were still not convinced and they gathered at the tabernacle to accuse Moses and Aaron of murdering the Levites. A cloud covered the tabernacle. Moses told Aaron to get his censer going and get among the crowd, "for there is wrath gone out from the Lord; and the plague is begun," which meant that people were dropping dead.

Aaron did as he was told and stood between the dead and the living, and the people ceased dying. On this occasion, 14,700 people died. Aaron then went back to Moses, who was standing in the entrance of the tabernacle, and no one else died.

THE ARK OF THE COVENANT AND OTHER SECRET WEAPONS OF THE ANCIENTS

WISDOM OF SOLOMON

AV "For when the dead were now fallen by heaps one upon another, standing between, he stayed the wroth, and parted the way to the living.

AV "For the long garment was the whole world, and in the four rows of stones was the glory of the fathers graven, and thy Majesty upon the diadem of his head.

AV "Unto these the destroyer gave place, and was afraid of them; for it was enough that they only tasted the wrath."

In "Worlds in Collision," Velikovsky attributes the opening of the ground to an earthquake. In the absence of any other explanation, this theory holds. However, his theory regarding the fire which came out from the Lord is less convincing. He claims that the heat from the censers ignited deposits of naphtha (or crude petroleum) in the cracks of the ground. Thousands of people were present, yet only the men carrying censers died.

It is not surprising that people who read the Bible today regard Moses as little more than a stage magician, for even those who were present at the time, and saw all these things take place, accused him of killing their fellows.

Probably, Moses foresaw that the multitude would gather against him and Aaron the following day; for there was little or nothing that he did not know. Once again, there was plenty of time to prepare.

In the Bible, "plague" is used to describe anything which resulted in mass illness or death, including leprosy and venereal disease. When the people gathered in front of the tabernacle, they began to fall dead. Aaron took up his censer and stood between the dead and the living. This implies that the people in the front fell first, and that the "plague" moved back through their ranks. There is no mention of fire.

THE ARK OF THE COVENANT AND OTHER SECRET WEAPONS OF THE ANCIENTS

Moses is described as being very meek, and, despite his spiritual powers, he would become upset when people doubted him. However, he was extremely well educated, for he was brought up as a prince of Egypt and would have received the best. Also, Moses was a prophet (or seer). He knew what would happen when the two-hundred and fifty men brought their censers. However, something even more devastating was required to convince the people. It is widely known that high priests contrived a variety of ingenious methods of deceiving the public. One such example is The Temple of the Sun which was at the base of the Sphinx. There, the priests made their voices echo in such a way that the Sphinx appeared to be talking. Moses, together with several famous philosophers, is known to have studied there.

On a material level, it is hard to believe that the ark was sufficiently powerful to cause the ground to open. The chasm was wide enough for three households to fall in and it closed up again after.

The Levites, who carried the censers, probably wore the same clothing as Aaron's sons but, as was demonstrated by the death of Nadab and Abihu, it afforded no protection when they carried brass implements, which attracted the electronic arc from the mercy seat. Aaron also had a brass censer, but he was wearing the clothing of high priest. The radiation seems to have been deflected by the stones in the breastplate which contained the Urim and Thummim. The stones consisted of

THE ARK OF THE COVENANT AND OTHER SECRET WEAPONS OF THE ANCIENTS

chalcedonies, christles, silicates, and corundums which are used today in the transmission of electricity and radio waves. Perhaps they created one of the negative force fields which are thought to exist, but about which little is known.

Throughout all this, Moses remained at the doorway of the tabernacle. Perhaps he turned off the power to give the impression that Aaron had halted the "plague."

The purple dye used in the curtains of the tabernacle was obtained from the gastropod mollusk. Squids exude Vanadium, some of which finds its way into shellfish. This means that there was probably Vanadium in the curtains which would produce radiation when bombarded by electrons.

In order to assert Aaron's entitlement to the office of high priest, and to leave no doubt in the minds of the rebels that the Levites were chosen to serve in the tabernacle, Moses collected a rod (or staff) from the leader of each of the twelve tribes. Aaron's name was placed on the rod of Levi. The rods were placed in front of the ark overnight. It was

said that the man whose rod blossomed would become the high priest. Needless to say, the rod of Levi grew buds, blossoms, and almonds. (Only Moses and Aaron were permitted to enter the inner sanctum.)

When the people saw that Aaron was still the boss, they were frightened. Obviously, they

THE ARK OF THE COVENANT AND OTHER SECRET WEAPONS OF THE ANCIENTS

thought that a change of leadership would result in the power of the ark being subdued so that less people died.

Aaron is again reminded that only he and his sons are permitted to enter the veil and go near to the altar, but the Levites were to serve in the tabernacle of the congregation. This passage ends with the much-repeated threat, "and the stranger that cometh nigh shall be put to death." The word "stranger" applied to any unauthorized person.

The secrets which were known to the high priests were never written down and were passed only to their successors. The original seventy Levites, who were chosen as elders, may have found out too much and thus have been in a position to take over the priesthood. Now that they, and the rest of the leaders, are dead, and the people have had the living daylights scared out of them, there will no doubt be peace in the camp for some time to come.

The camp moved to Kadesh, in the desert of Zin. Aaron's sister Miriam died. Many startling events followed, but only those connected with the ark will be dealt with here.

The camp moved to Mount Hor. Aaron died on the mount after Moses had stripped him of his high priest's garments and placed them on Aaron's son, Eleazar.

After many journeys and battles, camp was pitched in the land of Moab, where Moses died at the age of 120. He was succeeded by Joshua.

The Israelites were in the wilderness for forty years. During which time, their clothing did not wear out. Joshua was the only survivor of those who left Egypt.

It became the responsibility of Joshua, whom Moses had trained, to lead the people into the Promised Land.

He gave orders for them to prepare to pass over the river Jordan in three days time. The following morning, the camp moved to the banks

THE ARK OF THE COVENANT AND OTHER SECRET WEAPONS OF THE ANCIENTS

of Jordan. On the third day, the people were told that when they saw the Levites carrying the ark, they were to go after it, but they were to follow at least half a mile behind.

When the feet of the priests who bore the ark entered the water, the river ceased flowing. They waited in the middle of the riverbed till all of the Israelites had crossed to the walls of the city of Jericho. As soon as the feet of the priests reached the opposite bank, the river began to flow again.

When Moses led the Israelites out of Egypt, the waters of the Red

THE ARK OF THE COVENANT AND OTHER SECRET WEAPONS OF THE ANCIENTS

Sea parted, allowing them to cross during the night, and then closed upon the Egyptians who pursued them in the morning. The explorer, Frank S. de Haas, found in 1884 that the Red Sea could be parted in this way by a strong east wind at Ras Atakah. Moses probably knew of this phenomenon. (Exodus 14.21-30.)

"And Israel saw the great work which the Lord did upon the Egyptians; and the people feared the Lord, and believed in the Lord, and his servant Moses." (Exodus 14.31, KJV.)

In "Worlds in Collision," Velikovsky attributes the parting of the Red Sea to a passing comet. Also, he claims that the flow of the river Jordan was cut off when a slice of the riverbank fell away and formed a dam. (There were similar occurrences in 1267 and 1927.) He does not mention the ark. As the flow of the river ceased as soon as the Levites carrying the ark stepped into it, it can be assumed that the bank was cut by a laser beam. When the Levites left the river, it began flowing again, indicating that the same power was used to disintegrate the dam.

After crossing the Jordan, the Israelite males were circumcised. This was the first time that the operation had been performed since the exodus from Egypt. The text continues:

KJV "And the children of Israel encamped in Gilgal, and kept the Passover on the fourteenth day of the month at even in the plains of Jericho.

KJV "And they did eat of the old corn of the land on the morrow after the Passover, unleavened cakes, and parched corn in the selfsame day.

KJV "And the manna ceased on the morrow after they had eaten old corn of the land; neither had the children of Israel manna anymore; but they did eat of the fruit of the land of Canaan that year.

KJV "And it came to pass, when Joshua was by Jericho, that he

THE ARK OF THE COVENANT AND OTHER SECRET WEAPONS OF THE ANCIENTS

lifted up his eyes and looked, and, behold, there stood a man over against him with his sword drawn in his hand; and Joshua went unto him, and said unto him, Art thou for us, or for our adversaries?

KJV "And he said, Nay, but as the captain of the host of the Lord am I now come. And Joshua fell on his face to the earth, and did worship."

THE ARK OF THE COVENANT AND OTHER SECRET WEAPONS OF THE ANCIENTS

The cessation of the manna supply coincided with the arrival of the stranger who commanded reverence. This suggests that "the captain of the host of the Lord" took the machine away. According to "The Kabbalah Decoded," the manna machine was sometimes referred to as the "Lord" and the receptacles in which the manna formed were called "hosts." When first seen, forty years earlier, the manna was on the ground "round about the host."

When Joshua's men had recovered from the operation, they marched round the walls of Jericho (a distance of two miles) followed by seven priests blowing on trumpets and rams' horns. Behind them, the Levites carried the ark.

This was repeated on each of six days. On the seventh day, the procession went round seven times. Upon completing the seventh circuit, the priests blew on their trumpets, the people shouted, and "the wall fell down flat."

Excavations carried out by Dr. John Garstang between 1929 and 1936 reveal that the wall was double, the two walls being 15' apart; the outer wall, 6' thick; the inner wall 12' thick; both being about 30' high. They were built, not very substantially, on faulty, uneven foundations of brick, 4" thick and 1' to 2' long, laid in mud and mortar. The two walls were linked together by houses built across the top. Dr. Garstang found that the outer wall fell outward and down the hillside, dragging the inner wall and houses.

The soldiers, who stood round the wall waiting for it to fall, walked straight in. (Therefore, the fall of the wall was not, as Velikovsky claims, caused by an earthquake.) The invaders destroyed every living thing except Rahab and her relatives.

Rahab is described in the Bible as a harlot but she is more likely to have been an inn-keeper, for she later married a prince in Judah. She was saved in return for sheltering the two spies whom Joshua had sent into the city. She helped them to escape through a window of her house which was built on the wall. (The RSV states that the house was "in" the wall.) The spies gave her a piece of scarlet cord to place in the window from which she let them down.

THE ARK OF THE COVENANT AND OTHER
SECRET WEAPONS OF THE ANCIENTS

When the inhabitants of Jericho had been slaughtered, the two men who had acted as spies went into Rahab's house. This indicates that this portion of the wall did not fall.

A popular belief is that the high pitched frequency of the sound of the trumpets caused the wall to disintegrate. Although this is probably true, the laser beams directed at it during the thirteen circuits made by

THE ARK OF THE COVENANT AND OTHER SECRET WEAPONS OF THE ANCIENTS

the ark would have weakened the wall considerably. The length and thickness of the scarlet cord which was given to Rahab is not stated. It either repelled the powerful rays of the ark or acted as a signal to the Levites to turn it away when passing that part of the wall.

When the manna supply ceased, the Israelites ate old corn and fruit from Canaan. Nothing was taken from Jericho, where Dr. John Garstang's excavations revealed an abundance of wheat, barley, dates and lentils in the store rooms. This suggests that the radiation which weakened the walls also contaminated the food. Furthermore, Joshua ordered that no souvenirs were to be taken, but one man, Achan, took a garment (together with some silver and gold).

KJV "And Joshua, and all Israel with him, took Achan the son of Zerah, and the silver, and the garment, and the wedge of gold, and his sons, and his daughters, and his oxen, and his asses, and his sheep, and his tent, and all that he had; and they brought them unto the valley of Achor.

KJV "And Joshua said, 'Why hast thou troubled us? The Lord shall trouble thee this day.' And all Israel stoned him with stones, and burned him with fire, after they had stoned him with stones.

KJV "And they raised over him a great heap of stones."

Joshua obviously knew how dangerous radio active material could be.

Color seems to be associated with various forms of radiation from the ark. The veil in the tabernacle was purple and the dye may have contained Vanadium. Purple cloth was also used to cover the radioactive ashes from the altar. The red coloring of the rams' skins on the roof of the tabernacle was probably rust from iron ore. This would have added to the conductivity of the exterior tent. Most red (or scarlet) dye is obtained from a scale insect called scarlet-grain. In Amulets and Talismans, the author points out that red stones were believed to protect

THE ARK OF THE COVENANT AND OTHER SECRET WEAPONS OF THE ANCIENTS

the wearers from fire and lightning.

After the deaths of Moses and Aaron, the Israelites were not bothered again by the ark. This justifies the fear of the people when they knew that Aaron was to continue to hold office as high priest.

The ark is not mentioned again until the Israelites began losing battles against the Bengamites. They offered burnt offerings, but there were no spectacular events attributable to the ark. At that time Phinehas, the son of Eleazar, was the high priest.

THE ARK OF THE COVENANT AND OTHER SECRET WEAPONS OF THE ANCIENTS

During the time of the judges, the secrets of the ark's power seem to have been lost.

When the Israelites began losing battles against the Philistines, they moved the ark from Shiloh to their camp at Ebenezer. Eli was then high priest. He was dissatisfied with his two sons, Hophni and Phinehas, because they abused the priesthood by fornicating with the women who came to the tabernacle. It is therefore unlikely that he would have entrusted them with much knowledge of the ark.

Eli's ward, Samuel, was known to be a prophet but he was still a child.

The ark did not help the Israelites, and they were beaten by the Philistines, who captured the ark. Hophni and Phinehas died in the battle. When Eli heard the news, he fainted and broke his neck in the resultant fall. He was 98 and blind.

The Philistines took the ark to Ashdod and placed it in the House of Dagon. (The statue of Dagon, which the Philistines worshipped as a god, was a stone bust. Its hands were probably across its forehead, with the palms outwards.) In the morning, Dagon was found lying on his face near the ark. They picked him up and put him back in his place.

KJV "And when they arose early on the morrow-morning, behold, Dagon was fallen on his face to the ground before the ark of the Lord; and the head of Dagon and both the palms of his hands were cut off upon the threshold; only the stump of Dagon was left to him."

RSV "were lying cut off upon the threshold . . ."

After this, the inhabitants of Ashdod were stricken with hemorrhoids. These incurable hemorrhoids caused death. The men of Ashdod decided that they must get rid of the ark, so they took it to the city of Gath, where the same thing occurred. (The words, "they had the hemorrhoids in their secret parts," are in the KJV only and are not contained

THE ARK OF THE COVENANT AND OTHER SECRET WEAPONS OF THE ANCIENTS

in the original manuscript. Perhaps an early translator made a marginal note referring to the secret parts of the ark and this found its way into the wrong part of the text.)

Next, the ark was taken to Ekron, and this displeased the Ekronites. It was then decided to send the ark back to the Israelites.

KJV "And the men that died not were smitten by the hemorrhoids; and the cry of the city went up to heaven."

No deaths occurred when the Israelites moved the ark from Shiloh to Ebenezer, nor when the Philistines captured it and took it to Ashdod. A possible explanation is that Eli wisely rendered the ark safe whilst it was in his care, but when it fell into the hands of the Philistines, a Levite (or Eli's ward Samuel) sneaked into the House of Dagon with the intention of placing fragments of stone inside the ark. The first attempt to break Dagon failed but the second succeeded. The ark now emitted a different type of ray than before and thus caused both hemorrhoids and death. The RSV uses "tumors" instead of "hemorrhoids." Tumors can be caused by radiation.

The protective clothing which was made for Aaron and his sons included underpants.

"And thou shall make for them linen breeches to cover their nakedness; from the loins even unto the thighs they shall reach;

"And they shall be upon Aaron, and upon his sons, when they come into the tabernacle of the congregation, or when they come near unto the altar to minister in the holy place; that they bear not iniquity and die; it shall be a statute forever unto him and his seed after him." (Exodus 28.42 & 43, KJV.)

The Philistines kept the ark for seven months before returning it to the Israelites on a new cart drawn by two unguided cows. The cows pulled the cart to Bethshemesh and stopped in a field by a great stone.

THE ARK OF THE COVENANT AND OTHER SECRET WEAPONS OF THE ANCIENTS

The reapers rejoiced and made a burnt offering of the two contaminated cows. The Levites took the ark off the cart and placed it upon the stone, where the Bethshemites gathered to offer sacrifices. As a result of coming close to the ark, 50,070 of them died.

The RSV states that seventy (not 50,070) men died because they looked into the ark. However, the footnote explains that this is the opinion of the translators. It is unlikely that there would have been over 50,000 people at Bethshemesh. Events which occurred earlier in the history of the ark show that only a high priest, wearing protective clothing, could touch the ark and live. As only eight people could have looked into the ark at the same time, and those eight would have died instantly, it is highly improbable that another sixty-two men would have come after them to suffer the same fate. It is more reasonable to assume that seventy people became ill and subsequently died.

The ark was taken to Kirjathjearin and placed in the house of Abinadab. Eleazar, the son of Abinadab, was placed in charge of it. He obviously had more knowledge than the Levites who took it off the cart, for it remained there harmlessly for twenty years.

Upon the orders of King David, the ark was brought out of the house of Abinadab and placed on a newly made ox cart for transportation to Baalperazim. However, when the procession reached the threshing floor of Nachon, the ark shook violently on the cart. One of the men, Uzza, placed his hand on the ark to steady it and promptly died on the spot. (In those days a threshing floor was a piece of open ground.)

This incident displeased King David, and he was afraid to take the ark into his city, so he placed it in the house of Obededom (the Gittite), where it remained for three months. When David found out that Obededom's household was thriving despite the presence of the ark, he brought it into the city and placed it in the tabernacle which he had pitched for it.

THE ARK OF THE COVENANT AND OTHER SECRET WEAPONS OF THE ANCIENTS

When King David was known to be dying, his son Adonijah appointed himself king. When David found out, he proclaimed that his other son, Solomon, was to be made king, not Adonijah. Adonijah was now frightened of Solomon and took hold of the horns of the incense altar. In doing so, he appears to have attempted suicide.

KJV "And Solomon said, 'If he will shew himself a worthy man, there shall not be a hair of him fall to the earth; but if wickedness shall be found in him, he shall die.'"

Solomon expected Adonijah to die, but he did not.

So, after the death of their father, Solomon put Adonijah to death. He also expelled the priest, Abiathar. Joab, a follower of Abiathar, then became scared. He ran to the tabernacle and took hold of the horns of the incense altar.

"And Benaiah came to the tabernacle of the Lord, and said unto him, 'Thus saith the king, "Come forth."' And he said, 'Nay, but I will die here.'"

Joab obviously expected to die before the incense altar, but Solomon was less confident, for Adonijah survived when he tried the same thing.

Solomon ordered Joab to be put to death.

Four-hundred and eighteen years after the Israelites left Egypt, King Solomon began building his temple, where a special place was made for the ark. The temple took seven years to build. When it was finished, the ark and all the vessels were brought from the city of David and placed in the oracle of the temple. There was nothing in the ark then, except the two tablets of stone which Moses put in at Horeb. (Exodus 40.20)

King Uzziah decided to burn incense in the temple.

THE ARK OF THE COVENANT AND OTHER SECRET WEAPONS OF THE ANCIENTS

KJV "And Azariah the priest went after him, and with him four-score priests of the Lord, that were valiant men.

KJV "And they withstood Uzziah the king, and said unto him, 'It appertaineth not unto thee, Uzziah, to burn incense unto the Lord, but to the priests, the sons of Aaron, that are consecrated to burn incense, so go out of the sanctuary, for thou hast trespassed; neither shall it be for thine honor from the Lord God.'

KJV "Then Uzziah was wroth, and he had a censer in his hand to burn incense; and while he was wroth with the priests, the leprosy rose

THE ARK OF THE COVENANT AND OTHER SECRET WEAPONS OF THE ANCIENTS

up in his forehead in the house of the Lord, from beside the incense altar."

No mention is made of the ark, which would have been out of sight behind the veil of the oracle.

After arguing with Moses, Miriam, the sister of Aaron, became leprous at the tabernacle. (Numbers 12.10)

In 606 BC, King Nebuchadnezzar plundered Solomon's Temple and took some of the treasure, together with captives (including Daniel) to Babylon. The remainder of the treasure and more captives (includ-

THE ARK OF THE COVENANT AND OTHER SECRET WEAPONS OF THE ANCIENTS

ing Ezekiel, the priest) were taken in 597 BC. The prophet Jeremiah and others escaped to Egypt and appear to have taken the Ark of the Covenant with them, for it is not mentioned again in the OT. However, it reappears in the Apocrypha where Jeremiah is called Jeremy.

In the year 175 BC, Antiochus plundered the temple at Jerusalem and took away the incense altar, the candlestick, the table, the censers, the veil, the crowns, and everything else he could lay his hands on. (No mention is made of the ark.) Antiochus carried all the plunder off to his own land.

In the year 164 BC, Judas decided to cleanse and repair the temple on mount Sion. New vessels were made for the sanctuary; these included the candlestick, the table, the sacrificial altar, and the incense altar. (No mention is made of the ark.)

Simon, the son of Mattathais, was made governor and chief priest in 140 BC, and was placed in charge of the sanctuary.

The following is extracted from a letter sent to the Jews in Egypt of 124 BC:

AV "It is also contained in the same writing that the prophet, being warned of God, commanded the tabernacle and the ark to go with him, as he went forth into the mountain, where Moses climbed up, and saw the heritage of God.

AV "And when Jeremy came thither, he found a hollow cave, wherein he laid the tabernacle, and the ark, and the altar of incense, and so stopped the door.

AV "And some of those that followed him came to mark the way, but they could not find it.

AV "Which when Jeremy perceived, he blamed them saying, 'As for that place, it shall be unknown until the time that God gather his people again together, and receive them unto mercy.

THE ARK OF THE COVENANT AND OTHER SECRET WEAPONS OF THE ANCIENTS

AV "'Then shall the Lord shew them these things, and the glory of the Lord shall appear, and the cloud also, as it was shewed to Moses, and as when Solomon desired that the place might be honorably sanctified.'" (Exodus 40.34 and 35, 1 Kings 8.10 and 11)

This appears to be the end of the story. Jeremiah hid the Ark of the Covenant, confident that it would one day be found and restored to its former glory. However, an Ethiopian writing indicates that Jeremiah was misled and that the Ark which he attempted to preserve was not the original Ark, but a substitute that replaced it in Solomon's Temple.

THEFT OF THE ARK

News of the power and glory of King Solomon the Wise was spread afar by merchants. The Bible states that the Queen of Sheba could not believe what she heard and decided to pay Solomon a visit (1 Kings 10). She took a huge retinue and was entertained lavishly by the King. She left with many gifts, we are told.

Similarities between the Biblical account and that contained in the Nebra Nagast (translated by Sir E.A. Wallis Budge, London, 1932) leave little doubt that Queen Makeda of Ethiopia was also queen of

THE ARK OF THE COVENANT AND OTHER SECRET WEAPONS OF THE ANCIENTS

Sheba, who, nine months after returning to her own country, gave birth to a son, whom she named Bayna-lehkem.

At the age of 22, Bayna-lehkem paid a visit to his father. Although the delighted King lavished goods upon his son, the young man wanted only one thing — the Ark of the Covenant.

How could the King part with this priceless relic? It would cause a revolution if anyone found out that he had given it away. Wisdom prevailed. Solomon stipulated that his son could take the Ark provided that it was done in absolute secrecy and that he, the King, would have no official knowledge of the removal.

The clever Bayna-lehkem entered the "most holy" space of the temple and took the measurements of the Ark. He then had parts made which, when assembled, would resemble the original under the drapes. After making the switch one night, he set off with the precious gift to his mother, Queen Makeda.

The temple priests were not deceived for long. They discovered the theft and reported immediately to the King. Again, Solomon's unquestioned wisdom prevailed. He said that no one should be told that the Ark was no longer in the temple. The priests were told to embellish the substitute to make it look even more like the original.

The full details of this switch can be found in Erich von Daniken's "Signs of the Gods." Supposedly, the original Ark came to rest in the Ethiopian town of Axum. Ethiopia was occupied by foreign powers in 1936, so we can only speculate where the Ark of the Covenant may be now.

Poor Jeremiah!

THE OPERATION OF THE ARK

The original British edition of this book published a few years ago led me into contact with a variety of interesting people and publica-

THE ARK OF THE COVENANT AND OTHER SECRET WEAPONS OF THE ANCIENTS

tions which added to my knowledge of the Ark.

The first was an American, Bill Cox, who is a professional dowser and an expert on pyramids. Bill has made an in-depth study of the natural energy contained within square-based pyramid frames. The frames, which can be of any size, can be used for keeping cutting edges sharp, preserving food, curing illnesses, and growing better plants. From a friend in New Zealand I learned that a large pyramid frame in a back garden was being used to cure arthritis and other complaints for which doctors were unable to prescribe relief. Even a greyhound with a torn ligament, which a veterinary surgeon said would never race again, was cured after a spell inside the pyramid. It ran better than ever and became a hot favorite. The frames can be made from any material. (Apparently copper is best, but even cardboard models produce results.) The angles at the base must be 514.28570 (one seventh of 3600), and one side must be aligned with magnetic north. They need not be covered.

Many of the mysteries surrounding the Great Pyramid of Giza remain to be unraveled, but it is now known that it was never intended as a burial chamber. In addition to its function as a mystery school, the pyramid was a power house. The sarcophagus was used either to rejuvenate those who lay in it or to boost their cosmic awareness.

Other — perhaps all — shapes attract natural energy. The dunces' hat (or cone) placed by teachers on the head of a backward child may have originally been designed to stimulate mental processes. Witches and wizards are almost always characterized in conical hats, which brings to mind the story of the sorcerer's apprentice, who put on the magician's hat and was immediately endowed with power that he could not control.

It is all a question of using suitable antennae to attract the natural forces, and I feel that this was (at least partly) the principle on which the

THE ARK OF THE COVENANT AND OTHER SECRET WEAPONS OF THE ANCIENTS

Ark functioned.

Earth aerials, each of which keeps frost off one acre of trees, have been in use in some orchards in the United States for over thirty years, this according to Bruce Cathie in "Harmonic 288: The Pulse of the Universe." The aerials consist of a thirty foot central mast, up which (through insulating disks placed at intervals) run seven 10-gauge copper wires. At the top of the mast, the wires bend out horizontally with one pointing towards magnetic north and the others equidistant, thus forming the seventh angle. At the base of the mast, the same wires run eighteen inches under ground to radius 144 feet, where each coils round an alnico magnet before surfacing and bending back towards its other end at the top of the mast. Interestingly, there was a gold, seven-pronged lamp-holder in front of the Ark of the Covenant and that too may have been an antenna.

When Moses received the instructions for building the Ark and the tabernacle which was to house it, he was told exactly which materials and colors were to be used; there was to be no adulteration. Today, we haphazardly blend materials and colors in complete ignorance of the effects from natural forces. The buildings in which we live and work are probably counterproductive to receptivity and inspiration and thus aggravate illness and distress. Anyone who has sat for a time in an Indian teepee will attest to experiencing a strange feeling of peaceful calm. As yet, I have not met anyone who has been inside an igloo, but the same seems to be true of domed structures.

In the mid-1950's, a California man spent thousands of dollars on a 55 foot dome-shaped generator which he called the "Integratron," claiming that it generated ions in the same way as the Ark of the Covenant. The purpose of this device was rejuvenation, and the inventor hoped to be able to treat ten thousand people per day. Unfortunately, the man died before his work could be completed. Another machine, the Multiple Wave Oscillator, was invented by Georges Lakhovsky and

THE ARK OF THE COVENANT AND OTHER SECRET WEAPONS OF THE ANCIENTS

described in his book "The Secret of Life." His discovery that every cell in the body is a minute electrical generator convinced him that diseases and disorders are caused by cellular oscillatory disequilibrium. The apparatus he used for treatment consisted of two box-like units, one placed on each side of the patient, and between which a radio wave passed. Transistorization was not available to Lakhovsky, but improved, portable models of his equipment are being marketed in England.

Radionic therapy has advanced to the extent that the condition of a distant patient can apparently be diagnosed from a sample of hair, blood, urine, etc. The sample enables the apparatus to "tune in" to the wavelength of the patient, thus enabling treatment to restore cellular equilibrium to be transmitted.

What has all this to do with the Ark of the Covenant? Firstly, it demonstrates that even the simplest antennae can be used to direct natural energy in a beneficial way, and secondly, that to be fully understood these phenomena require knowledge of more than one scientific subject.

A secondary effect of treatment with the Lakhovsky device is that the patients are said to be rejuvenated. George Van Tassel's "Integratron," which we mentioned earlier, was to have been used for that purpose, as was the sarcophagus in the Great Pyramid. I have even found a hint that perhaps the Ark of the Covenant was used for rejuvenation. During the forty years that the Israelites were in the wilderness, their shoes and clothing did not wear out (Deuteronomy 29.5). Also, when Moses died at the age of 120, "his eye was not dim, nor his natural force abated." (Deuteronomy 34.7). Perhaps Moses earned this splendid epitaph as a result of rejuvenation by the ark. The same may be true of King Solomon's virility. He had seven hundred wives and three hundred concubines (1 Kings 11.3). When visited by the Queen of Sheba, he was at the height of his power (1 Kings 10) and, according to the Nebra Kabast, he entertained Banya-lehkam (his son) in lavish style 23

THE ARK OF THE COVENANT AND OTHER SECRET WEAPONS OF THE ANCIENTS

years later. However, after the removal of the ark by his son, Solomon lost his wisdom and his power. He no longer had control over his women and, for the first time, is described as "old." (1 Kings 11.4).

Solomon's temple consisted of two rooms and a porch. The Ark of the Covenant was in the "most holy" space (a thirty foot cube), under the wings of two huge cherubim. Stairs led down from the windowless "most holy" space to the incense altar in the "holy" space, which, unlike the original tabernacle, contained ten, instead of one, seven-pronged lamp-holders and tables of shewbread. The porch was flanked by two freestanding pillars, twenty-seven feet high, six feet in diameter, topped with ornate chapiters, and called Jachin and Boaz.

Outside the temple, five elaborate lavers with wheeled bases were placed on the north side and five on the south. At the foot of the steps from the porch stood the sacrificial altar, fifteen feet high with a thirty foot square base, and the most curious item of all, the "sea," a huge water tank which probably weighed over twenty-five tons and contained almost 10,000 gallons, and stood on twelve oxen. (See diagram 6.)

There were three tiers of small rooms built against the north, west and south walls. They were five cubits high and seven cubits broad in the top tier, six in the middle, and five in the bottom. As yet, no one has dared to suggest that the rooms were used for anything other than storage (1 Kings 5-8 and 2 Chronicles 3 & 4).

Bruce Cathie, airline pilot and author of "Harmonic 288: Pulse of the Universe," shares my opinion that the "sea" was a parabolic dish and he gave me diagram 8 containing his calculations. When functioning, the apparatus may have made a noise like the sea. Also, a researcher whom I once met is of the opinion that the "sea" was used for rejuvenation. The replicas in the Mormon temples are called "baptismal fonts."

The combined skills of many scientists and engineers would be necessary to rediscover the technology which was available to the ancients. There are rumors that some progress has been made, but the knowledge is withheld for the personal use of the research financiers. An attempt to separate religion from myth is being made by the newly formed Society for the Interpretation of Ancient Texts, 10 Stonehill Court, Suite 511, Scarborough, Ontario, Canada M1W 2X8. The introductory pamphlet to prospective members states that in the Bible, forty-eight different Hebrew words have been translated as "fire."

In conclusion, I believe it has become apparent that so-called ancient people had available to them knowledge that has since been lost to the world. It would benefit everyone to rediscover some of this ancient technology, for by combining modern science and ancient methods it should be possible to solve fuel and energy problems and create a pollution-free environment.

THE ARK OF THE COVENANT AND OTHER SECRET WEAPONS OF THE ANCIENTS

Moses' staff turns into a serpent and devours the other serpent.

THE ARK OF THE COVENANT AND OTHER SECRET WEAPONS OF THE ANCIENTS

Moses' serpent-staff frightens the court of Pharoah.

THE ARK OF THE COVENANT AND OTHER SECRET WEAPONS OF THE ANCIENTS

Moses encounters the "burning bush."

THE ARK OF THE COVENANT AND OTHER
SECRET WEAPONS OF THE ANCIENTS

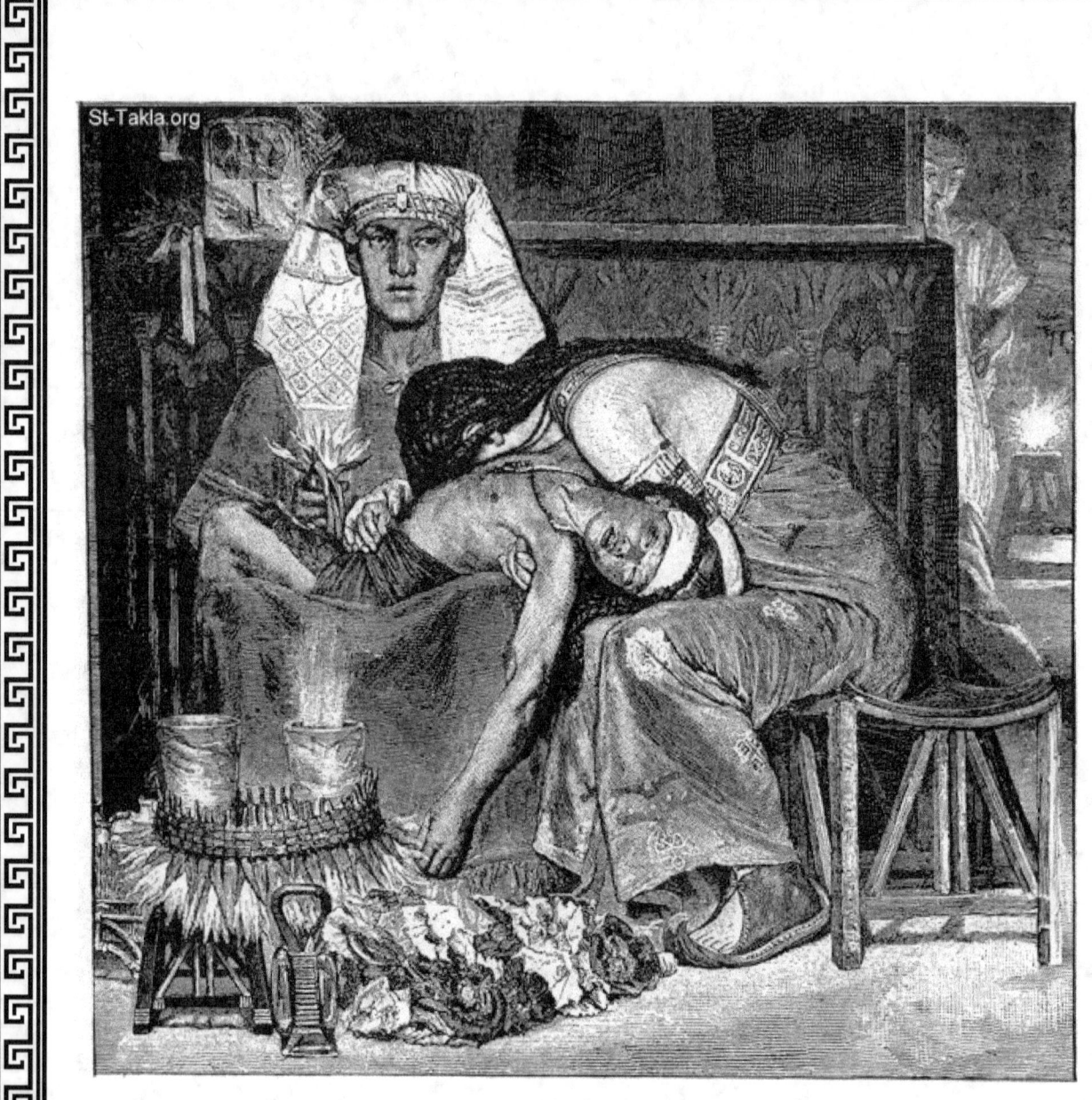

After Pharoah's young son dies, he agrees to let the Jews leave Egypt.

THE ARK OF THE COVENANT AND OTHER SECRET WEAPONS OF THE ANCIENTS

The fleeing Jews are stopped by the Red Sea.

THE ARK OF THE COVENANT AND OTHER SECRET WEAPONS OF THE ANCIENTS

THE ARK OF THE COVENANT AND OTHER SECRET WEAPONS OF THE ANCIENTS

Hardship and death await the Jews in the wilderness.

THE ARK OF THE COVENANT AND OTHER SECRET WEAPONS OF THE ANCIENTS

In Moses' absence, the Jews melted down the gold they had stolen from the Egyptians and molded a golden calf, which they worshipped.

THE ARK OF THE COVENANT AND OTHER SECRET WEAPONS OF THE ANCIENTS

Unable to control his anger, Moses destroys the Commandments.

THE ARK OF THE COVENANT AND OTHER SECRET WEAPONS OF THE ANCIENTS

THE ARK OF THE COVENANT AND OTHER SECRET WEAPONS OF THE ANCIENTS

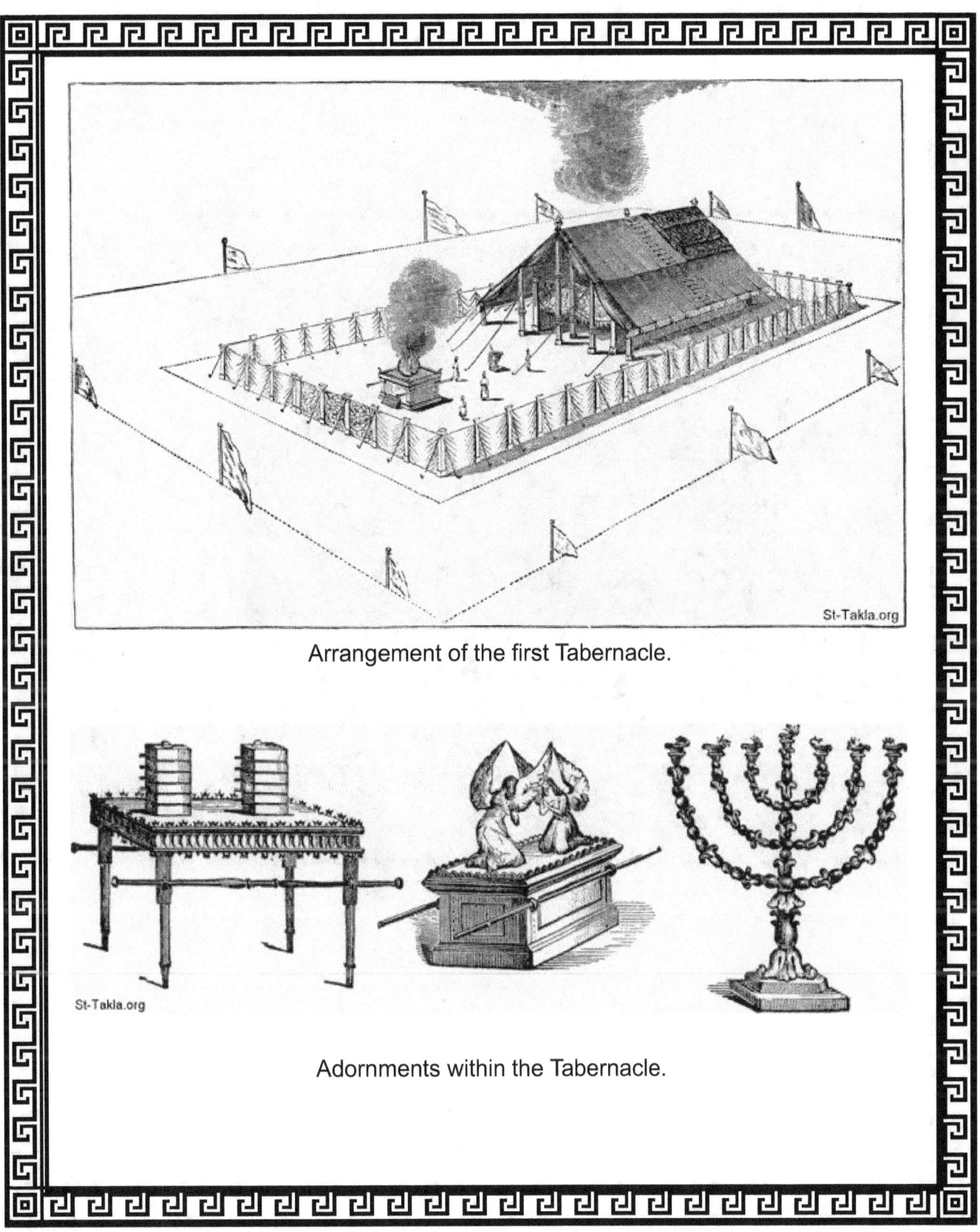

Arrangement of the first Tabernacle.

Adornments within the Tabernacle.

THE ARK OF THE COVENANT AND OTHER SECRET WEAPONS OF THE ANCIENTS

The protective clothing worn by the priests.

THE ARK OF THE COVENANT AND OTHER SECRET WEAPONS OF THE ANCIENTS

THE ARK OF THE COVENANT AND OTHER SECRET WEAPONS OF THE ANCIENTS

Aaron's rod buds and produces almonds, making him the new priest.

THE ARK OF THE COVENANT AND OTHER
SECRET WEAPONS OF THE ANCIENTS

The Jews are homeless vagabonds for 40 years.

THE ARK OF THE COVENANT AND OTHER
SECRET WEAPONS OF THE ANCIENTS

When the Ark is moved, the people must follow far behind, "lest they die."

THE ARK OF THE COVENANT AND OTHER SECRET WEAPONS OF THE ANCIENTS

Those who get close to the Ark soon sicken and die.

THE ARK OF THE COVENANT AND OTHER SECRET WEAPONS OF THE ANCIENTS

The Jews gather near the tel upon which is the city of Jericho.

THE ARK OF THE COVENANT AND OTHER SECRET WEAPONS OF THE ANCIENTS

The horror-stricken residents of Jericho flee their destroyed city.

THE ARK OF THE COVENANT AND OTHER SECRET WEAPONS OF THE ANCIENTS

Rehab lets down a scarlet cord so the two spys can escape after the walls of Jericho have fallen.

THE ARK OF THE COVENANT AND OTHER SECRET WEAPONS OF THE ANCIENTS

With Jericho destroyed, the way was open to Caanan

THE ARK OF THE COVENANT AND OTHER SECRET WEAPONS OF THE ANCIENTS

EPILOGUE

The history of the ark indicates that whilst it was in the tabernacle it produced both radiation and electricity, sometimes simultaneously. When out of the tabernacle, it emitted only radiation and was at times rendered safe. However, it could still build up a static charge whilst being transported, for Uzza was electrocuted when he placed his hand on it. A parabola was formed by the wings of the two cherubim above the ark. Laser beams were probably used on the walls of Jericho and also to form the dam in the river Jordan and disintegrate it again. Had the two tablets which Moses placed in the ark not been stone, but plutonium and uranium, it would definitely have been a nuclear reactor. This does not mean that the two plates could not still have been capacitors. Alternatively, the capacitors could have been the internal and external gold coverings of the wooden box. Although the ark was an electric cell, there appears to be no answer to the question of how it was capable of producing more than two volts.

Almost all of this book was written prior to the publication of "Deus est machina?" though I amended my text to include the manna-making machine. The article ends with the suggestion that the plans of the ark originated from an extraterrestrial source. At that time, my attention was drawn to another article, "The Ark of the Israelites was an Electrical Machine," by Dr. Bernard Finch, published in "Flying Saucer Review" May/June 1965. It appears to Dr. Finch that the Jewish high priests obtained the secret of the electrostatic machine from aliens. Also, I have

THE ARK OF THE COVENANT AND OTHER
SECRET WEAPONS OF THE ANCIENTS

found biblical evidence that this was the case. Surely we cannot all be wrong. Moses was given the original two tablets on which the commandments (or instructions) were written. To avoid creating problems, I left out the evidence that, in addition to everything else, the ark was a two-way radio. The "Lord" spoke from the mercy seat where the two cherubim acted as loud speakers. The Kabbalah contains unquestionable evidence that the ark was used to transmit prayers to the gods.

The mysterious Urim and Thummim may also have been given to Moses. Scattered references throughout various books suggest that they were connected with communication. This confirms my opinion that when they were placed behind the jewels in the breastplate of judgment which Aaron wore, the garment became a remote control panel.

The prophet Jeremiah carefully hid the ark in the 2,643 foot mountain, Nebo. The grave of Moses is thought to be in the same mountain. With modern equipment, it should be possible for the ark to be found. However, it would be advisable for the leader of any such expedition to consider the destructive history which is recorded in the OT.

According to the prophet Jeremiah, the ark will not be found until God gathers his people together again. (2 Macc 2.7) When he hid the ark, he was confident that it would one day be found.

When I began writing this monograph it was not my intention to prove anything. I merely wished to tell the complete story and draw attention to possibilities. Many questions remain unanswered, and I hope that, as a result of this publication, other individuals will become interested in the subject and make the results of their research available as I have done.

THE ARK OF THE COVENANT AND OTHER SECRET WEAPONS OF THE ANCIENTS

BIBLIOGRAPHY

Budge, Sir E.A. Wallis. "Amulets and Talismans" Collier Books, New York.

Finch, Dr. Bernard. "The Ark of the Israelites was an Electrical Machine." Flying Saucer Review. May/June 1965

Sassoon, George and Dale, Rodney. "Deus est machina?" New Scientist. 1 April 1976 "The Manna-Machine." Sidgwick & Jackson, London. "The Kabbalah Decoded." Duckworth & Co. Ltd. London.

Velikovsky, Immanuel. "Worlds in Collision." Victor Gollancz Ltd., London.

Von Daniken, Erich. "Chariots of the Gods" / "Signs of the Gods?" Souvenir Press Ltd., London.

The author welcomes correspondence addressed to him at 6 Grant Court, 18 Spencer Hill, London SW19 4NY, England.

THE ARK OF THE COVENANT AND OTHER SECRET WEAPONS OF THE ANCIENTS

WEAPONS OF MASS DESTRUCTION

IN ANCIENT INDIA

By Sean Casteel

The Ark of the Covenant was a formidable weapon indeed, as one learns when reading David Medina's in-depth discussion. But there is another form of ancient weaponry recorded in the myths and religious literature of ancient India that may strike some as even more formidable: the vimana, a flying craft that also carried weapons capable of the same kind of mass destruction as our present day nuclear and chemical weapons.

THE ARK OF THE COVENANT AND OTHER SECRET WEAPONS OF THE ANCIENTS

David Hatcher Childress has been studying vimanas for many years. His 2013 book, "Vimana: Flying Machines of the Ancients," is a worthy place to begin one's own study of the mysterious craft – be they manmade or of otherworldly origin – and the instruments of death they took aloft with them.

Childress explains that most of our current knowledge of the vimanas comes from ancient Indian religious writings, specifically the "Ramayana" and the "Mahabharata." The "Mahabharata" is a series of 18 books that includes an abbreviated version of the "Ramayana" as part of its story-in-a-story writing style. However, the "Ramayana" is really a completely separate book, and the events recounted therein take place before the battles detailed in the "Mahabharata." In any case, in a way similar to our current knowledge of the Ark of the Covenant, we are basically limited to religious texts as opposed to other forms of "proof."

In both the "Ramayana" and the "Mahabharata," the storylines "are centered on the complicated marriage and betrothal issues in ancient India and the dynastic succession of royal families in the many kingdoms – a collection of ancient states that were advanced in technology and culture," Childress writes.

All Hindus and Buddhists, over a billion people, know the story told in the "Ramayana," which Childress synopsizes thusly: "It is an entertaining and amazing story of dynastic succession: who is going to marry whom; who is going to be next in line to be king; and who gets to drive the hot-rod vimana to either steal the hot chicks or get them back. It has all the elements of the soap opera where the main characters own some sort of flight/airline companies that use their fleet of aircraft (which are armed with weapons) to fly around the world while they carry on their sexual shenanigans and aristocratic rivalries involving status and family disputes and duty. In fact, in both the 'Ramayana' and the 'Mahabharata,' the bad guys aren't really that bad at all, but just dutiful princes who adore Lord Shiva but do things their own way, including grabbing the women they want.''

It is difficult to determine just when these ancient Sanskrit texts were first written down or to ascertain the even earlier time period when the alleged historical events took place. Some historians place it as recently as 600 B.C., when Iron Age India is said to have appeared on the world stage, while others argue that it was some thousands of years prior. Childress contends that it is more convenient and likely more accurate to say it happened in an era of "prehistory" that we can pinpoint only vaguely and without confidence.

WHAT IS A VIMANA?

THE ARK OF THE COVENANT AND OTHER SECRET WEAPONS OF THE ANCIENTS

Having briefly described the ancient sources for our modern understanding of the vimanas, we will next examine just what the flying craft actually were.

"The ancient Indians themselves," writes Childress, "apparently wrote entire flight manuals on the control of various types of vimanas, of which there were as many as five different types, including: the Pushpaka vimana; the Shakuna vimana; the Sundara vimana; the Rukma vimana; and the Tripura vimana."

The "Ramayana" said that the Pushpaka vimana "resembles the Sun" and is "that aerial and excellent chariot going everywhere at will, that chariot resembling a bright cloud in the sky." Rama the king boarded the craft and "the excellent chariot rose up into the higher atmosphere."

Childress quotes British/American author and researcher Ivan T. Sanderson regarding ancient technological texts given the name "Manusa."

"It is from these authenticated texts," Sanderson writes, "mostly in poetic form, that some truly astonishing concepts have been derived. Poetic they may be; and nothing more than myth, legend or folklore, but they make statements that are more than just surprising. Several are couched in perfectly straightforward terms and are stated not to be legendary but technological, and thus called 'Manusa.' These are said by the writers to explain how certain devices were constructed for aerial flight, but not how to so construct them because the inventors and the establishment did not want such things to be mass-produced and get into the hands of any other than the rulers, commonly called 'kings' and 'princes.' What is more, there would appear to be more than ample suggestion, if not evidence, that such airships could be and were put to the most gruesome and devastating use in wartime."

Sanderson next quotes Desmond Leslie, whose name will be familiar to those acquainted with the story of UFO contactee George Adamski, who co-authored with Leslie the 1953 classic "Flying Saucers Have Landed." Leslie himself refers to a passage in an ancient text called the "Samarangana Sutrahara" that reads:

"Strong and durable must the body be made, like a great flying bird, of light material. Inside it one must place the mercury-engine with its iron heating apparatus beneath. By means of the power latent in the mercury which sets the driving whirlwind in motion, a man sitting inside may travel a great distance in the sky in a most marvelous manner. One can build a vimana as large as the temple of the God-in-motion. The vimana develops thunder power through the mercury and at once becomes a pearl in the sky. It develops power with the roar of a lion."

THE ARK OF THE COVENANT AND OTHER SECRET WEAPONS OF THE ANCIENTS

The "Ramayana" describes a vimana as a double-deck, circular or cylindrical aircraft with portholes and a dome that flew with the "speed of the wind" and gave forth a "melodious sound," which, Childress speculates, may have been a humming noise. Still another Indian text says a vimana is "an aerial car made of light wood looking like a great bird with a durable and well-formed body. It has two re-splendent wings and is propelled by air. It flies in the atmospheric re-gions for a great distance and carries several persons along with it. The inside construction resembles heaven created by Brahma himself. Iron, copper, lead and other metals are also used for these machines."

That last description, which mentions "two resplendent wings," sounds very much like our own airplanes, while the circular or cylin-drical craft mentioned in the "Ramayana" call to mind common shapes reported by UFO witnesses since the mid-20th century. The point to keep

THE ARK OF THE COVENANT AND OTHER SECRET WEAPONS OF THE ANCIENTS

in mind when discussing vimanas, however, is that, according to the Sanskrit traditions, the vimanas are both built and piloted by human beings. This differentiates them from other legends of ancient flying machines, such as "the pillar of fire," which led Moses and the Israelites, or the "chariot of fire" that took Elijah away. Those and numerous similar Biblical examples involve flying craft created by God and piloted by his angelic minions and are not within the technological capabilities of the human characters in the Judaic stories.

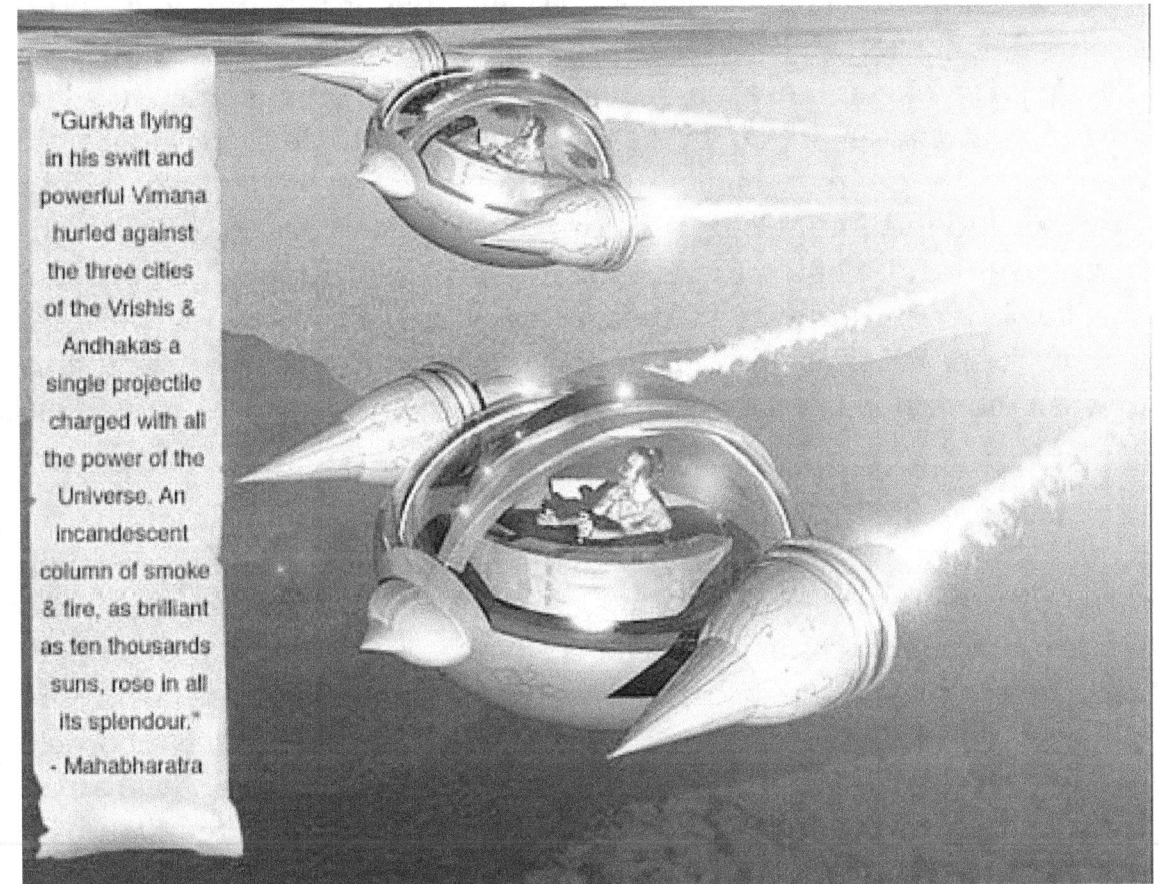

"Gurkha flying in his swift and powerful Vimana hurled against the three cities of the Vrishis & Andhakas a single projectile charged with all the power of the Universe. An incandescent column of smoke & fire, as brilliant as ten thousands suns, rose in all its splendour."
- Mahabharatra

THE FEARSOME "BRAHMASTRA" WEAPON

Early in "Vimana: Flying Machines of the Ancients," Childress discusses a weapon described in the "Mahabharata" and said to have been

THE ARK OF THE COVENANT AND OTHER SECRET WEAPONS OF THE ANCIENTS

used in the Kuruhshetra War, which was a series of four battles fought by rival families that Childress compares to both Armageddon and the American Civil War. A fantastic weapon known as a "Brahmastra" is used by the Pandava princes to decisively end their war against the Kaurava clan. The Brahmastra is similar to a super-missile with an atomic warhead.

This is a quote from Book Eight of the "Mahabharata":

"Gurkha, flying in his swift and powerful vimana, hurled a single projectile charged with all the power in the universe. An incandescent column of smoke and fire, as brilliant as a thousand suns, rose in all its splendor. It was an unknown weapon, an iron thunderbolt, a gigantic messenger of death, which reduced to ashes the entire race of the Vrishnis and the Andhakas. The corpses were so burned as to be unrecognizable. The hair and nails fell out; pottery broke without cause; and the birds turned white. After a few hours, all foodstuffs were infected. To escape from this fire, the soldiers threw themselves in streams to wash themselves and their equipment."

The text offers us certain clues to enable us to compare the Brahmastra to the nuclear missiles of our present time. The ancient projectile is said to be "charged with all the power in the universe," which instantly recalls the splitting of the atom, the primary component of all matter/power in the universe. The column of "smoke and fire, as brilliant as a thousand suns" can easily be correlated with a mushroom cloud, rising in all its "splendor." The burned corpses, the way people's hair and nails fell out, and the contamination of the food supply, are also well-known consequences of the radiation-saturated aftermath of a nuclear blast.

Interestingly, unlike the vimanas, the Brahmastra was said to have been devised not by mankind but by the Hindu creator god Brahma, who intended that the weapon be used in defense of his holy principles.

THE ARK OF THE COVENANT AND OTHER SECRET WEAPONS OF THE ANCIENTS

The Brahmastra never missed its mark and had to be used with very specific intent against an individual enemy or army, who would be completely annihilated. According to ancient beliefs, the weapon was obtained by meditating on the Lord Brahma and could only be used once in a lifetime. A great deal of mental concentration was required before the weapon was invoked and given to the user.

Brahma also created an even more powerful weapon, the Brahmashira, which had four times the power of the Brahmastra. The weapon was believed to cause severe environmental damage. The land became barren and both women and men became infertile. Drought-like conditions followed quickly; the rainfall ceased and cracks appeared in the tortured earth.

A WAR STORY FOR THE AGES

There are many examples of the use of the Brahmashira in Indian mythology, but one particularly compelling story involves an armed conflict between two mortals named Ashwatthama and Arjuna. Ashwatthama did not have his bow and arrow near him as Arjuna approached him, so he took a piece of straw, invoked the proper phrase required by Lord Brahma (or otherwise activated a Brahmashira with some special Brahma-inspired code) and then threw the straw at Arjuna. The straw now carried the power of the Brahmashira.

Arjuna did the same, invoking the Brahmashira to counter that of Ashwatthama. However, the collision of two Brahmashira's would have destroyed the universe, so mythic entities called the Rishi Vyas came between the two weapons bodily, thus blocking their collision. Arjuna managed to call back his Brahmashira, but Ashwatthama lacked that ability, so he commanded his weapon to attack the unborn grandchild of Arjuna, Parikshit, who was later rescued by the god-like powers of Krishna.

THE ARK OF THE COVENANT AND OTHER SECRET WEAPONS OF THE ANCIENTS

EVIDENCE OF AN ANCIENT NUCLEAR WAR

Childress points out that there is archeological evidence for this sort of mass destruction through warfare. Excavations of cities in the Indus Valley region, which includes parts of present day India and Pakistan, were conducted in the first half of the 20th century. Archeologists there uncovered evidence that the cities had been completely destroyed, with people lying dead in the streets. Some kind of "sudden doom" had decimated these cities, killing the entire population and leaving no survivors to bury the dead.

'India had a superior civilisation'

But Childress is, of course, not alone in interpreting the archeological data in that way. On a website called "UK Essays," an unknown writer makes reference to recent discoveries of green glass and many radioactive samples in certain excavations in India which are believed to have been associated with the "Mahabharata" war. Green glass is said to result when sand melts at very high temperatures, such as would be the case in a nuclear explosion.

"Another curious sign of an ancient nuclear war in India," the essay continues, "is a giant crater near Bombay. The nearly circular, 2,154-meter-diameter Lonar crater, aged at less than 50,000 years old, could be related to nuclear warfare in antiquity. No trace of any meteoric material, etc., has been found at the site or in the vicinity, and this is the world's only known 'impact' crater in basalt."

THE ARK OF THE COVENANT AND OTHER SECRET WEAPONS OF THE ANCIENTS

At another location in India, called Rajasthan, a layer of radioactive ash was found that covered a three-square mile area. An investigation into the ash was ordered after a very high rate of birth defects and cancer developed in the area. The levels of radiation registered so high on investigators' gauges that the Indian government cordoned off the region. Scientists then unearthed an ancient city where they found evidence of an atomic blast dating back 8,000 to 12,000 years.

"The blast was said to have destroyed most of the buildings," the essayist writes, "and probably a half-million people. Archeologist Francis Taylor stated that etchings in some nearby temples he translated suggested that they prayed to be spared from the great light that was coming to lay ruin to the city."

The essayist also touches on the same excavations referred to by Childress, conducted at the ancient Indian cities of Harappa and Mohenjo-Daro. Skeletons were discovered scattered throughout, many holding hands and sprawling in the streets as if some instant, horrible doom had taken place. The skeletons have been dated as thousands of years old and yet are among the most radioactive ever found, on par with those at Hiroshima and Nagasaki. At one site, Soviet researchers found a skeleton with a radioactive level 50 times greater than normal.

A LEONINE ROAR

Yet another Sanskrit scripture seems to point to the use of nuclear weapons in ancient India. As quoted by writer Colin Mulligan, on the website "UFO Evidence," a sampling of the sacred book the "Drona Parava" reads:

"Encompassed by many bowmen, Bhisma, smiting the while and uttering a leonine roar, took up and hurled at them with great force a fierce mace [weapon] of destruction of hostile ranks. The mace, of adamantine [extremely hard or unyielding] strength, hurled like Indra's thunder by Indra himself, crushed, O King, thy soldiers in battle. And it

THE ARK OF THE COVENANT AND OTHER SECRET WEAPONS OF THE ANCIENTS

THE ARK OF THE COVENANT AND OTHER
SECRET WEAPONS OF THE ANCIENTS

seemed to fill the whole earth with a loud noise. And blazing forth in splendor, that fierce mace inspired thy sons with fear. Beholding that mace of impetuous [violent] force and endowed with lightning flashes coursing towards them, thy warriors fled away uttering frightful cries. And at the unbelievable sound of that fiery mace, many fell down where they stood and many vimana warriors also fell down from their craft."

One is reminded of the Pentagon's use of the phrase "shock and awe" when describing the 1991 invasion of Iraq. The author of "Drona Parava" certainly boasts of the fear instilled in the enemy by Bhisma, the warrior king wielding the truly horrifying weapon that so lay waste the courage of his enemies.

There are further verses along those same lines.

"The sun seemed to turn around. The universe, scorched with heats, seemed to be in a fever. The elephants and other creatures of the land, scorched by the energy of the weapon, ran in fright, breathing heavily and desirous of protection against that terrible force."

The same passage continues: "A thick gloom suddenly shrouded the host. All points of the compass also were enveloped by that darkness. Rakshashas and Vicocha, crowding together, uttered fierce cries. Inauspicious winds began to blow."

That last section may be a reference to a "nuclear winter" occurring in the aftermath of the battle, a pollution of the atmosphere that could last for decades, centuries, or even millennia after the initial attack. We are reminded that the dangers of nuclear war lie not only in the death-dealing radiation release but also in the ruination of the environment, as mentioned in the passages on the Brahmastra and the Brahmahsira weapons earlier in this chapter.

And Mulligan supplies us with still more relevant scriptures, this time by way of Erich von Daniken's 1977 book, "According To The Evidence," in which von Daniken quotes these verses from the

THE ARK OF THE COVENANT AND OTHER SECRET WEAPONS OF THE ANCIENTS

"Mahabharata":

"The heavens cried out, the earth bellowed an answer, lightning flashed forth, fire flamed upwards, it rained down death. The brightness vanished, the fire was extinguished. Everyone who was struck by the lightning was turned to ashes. It was a ghastly sight to see. The corpses of the fallen were so mutilated they no longer looked like human beings. Never before have we seen such an awful weapon, and never before have we heard of such a weapon."

WHENCE COME THESE MIGHTY WEAPONS?

In his book "Gods and Spacemen In The Ancient Far East," the esteemed writer W.R. Drake comments that the warrior heroes in the "Mahabharata" appeared "to possess an arsenal of diverse, sophisticated nuclear weapons equal to, perhaps surpassing, the missiles of the Americans and Russians today." Drake also comments that certain Sanskrit passages bear "an uncanny resemblance to future wars, when our earth's capitals may be blasted with bombs of anti-matter launched from space satellites."

Having established the credibility of the existence of these ancient nukes and other high-tech weapons of mass destruction in the religious myth of ancient India, we must again ask the question, how did the presumably more primitive denizens of those times create them? According to Drake and von Daniken, they didn't invent them at all. The weapons were simply handed down to these ancient people by the gods or, in other words, highly advanced extraterrestrial "spacemen."

This "gift" of devastating weaponry can be viewed as highly irresponsible on the part of the extraterrestrials, something akin to giving a loaded gun to a small child and telling him "to go and play." But as we saw previously in this chapter, the weapons were said to have been created by the Hindu god Brahma for his own sacred purposes, and the mortal warrior who sought to deploy the devices could obtain them only

THE ARK OF THE COVENANT AND OTHER SECRET WEAPONS OF THE ANCIENTS

after much sincere meditation and prayer. Whatever ancient astronauts imparted these instruments of death likely also regulated closely both their use and "misuse."

There is also the "cyclical theory" of human history to consider. Perhaps mankind is doomed to repeatedly reach a level of technological sophistication that ultimately leads to its complete destruction. This idea is familiar from the myths of Atlantis, for example, and perhaps the nuclear winter described in the Indian myth quoted above describes the self-annihilation of that civilization. Are we nearing the end of our own brief "cycle," to be replaced by some future civilization, as yet undreamed of, that will also inevitably invent its doom?

J. Robert Oppenheimer, the nuclear physicist credited with creating the atomic bomb, was once asked how he felt about being the first to have achieved such a powerful weapon. He is said to have replied that he was only the first to have done so "in modern times." Oppenheimer openly believed that the "Mahabharata" contained within it tales of ancient nuclear weapons that preceded his own invention by many thousands of years. He had simply "rediscovered" what a vastly more archaic time had already known.

Again, as with the Ark of the Covenant, we are confronted with the notion that ancient man possessed technological abilities far beyond what we normally credit to him. A closer reading of both the Bible and the Hindu scriptures teaches us that the characters that populate these sacred pages were no strangers to powers that we take for granted today. Ancient man could not only fly but also wage aerial warfare through some combination of human invention and godly intervention, and even our present-day nuclear arsenals are nothing new under the sun.

MORE WEAPONRY OF THE BIBLICAL GOD

Was the Ark of the Covenant the only weapon of the Biblical God?

THE ARK OF THE COVENANT AND OTHER SECRET WEAPONS OF THE ANCIENTS

The answer to that question is an emphatic "No."

While it is commonly understood that UFOs or flying saucers are seen frequently in the pages of the Bible, what is perhaps less frequently mentioned is the deployment of these UFOs in warfare and their use as a weapon in the arsenal of the heavenly ones.

In an interview I conducted with researcher, writer and television personality Gary Stearman, of the "Prophecy In The News" ministry, based in Oklahoma City, he carefully explained how Biblical UFOs appeared in defense of Israel in ancient times and have reappeared in our own time.

THE CHARIOTS OF WONDER

"First of all," Stearman said, "the Bible speaks of fiery chariots. The chariot in Hebrew is called the 'merkavah.' Several modern Israelis have suggested that UFOs in the Hebrew be called 'merkavah mophtim.' And 'mophtim' means 'wonder.' So what you have in the Hebrew would be 'chariots of wonder' or 'vehicles of wonder.'"

Stearman made reference to a story in the Bible, from Second Kings, Chapter Six, beginning with verse fifteen.

"And when the servant of the man of God was risen early and gone forth," Stearman read aloud, "Behold, an host – that's an army – encompassed the city, both with horses and chariots. And his servant said unto him – of course, 'him' being Elisha – the servant said unto him, 'Alas, my master, how shall we do?' In other words, we are in deep trouble. And Elisha answered, 'Fear not, for they that be with us are more than they that be with them.' And Elisha prayed and said, 'Lord, I pray thee, open his eyes that he may see.' And the Lord opened the eyes of the young man, who saw and, behold, the mount was full of horses and chariots of fire round about Elisha."

Stearman then illuminated the text a bit more.

THE ARK OF THE COVENANT AND OTHER SECRET WEAPONS OF THE ANCIENTS

"Now what was going on here," he explained, "is that there was a great battle being fought in which Israel was threatened, deeply threatened. And the prophet Elisha went out on behalf of Israel. The king of Syria had invaded Israel, and Elisha went down to deliver God's message to the leaders of Israel. And he had a servant with him. The servant was deathly afraid that they were going to be killed, and Elisha prayed and the servant's eyes were opened. The servant was able to see that the Israelites were surrounded by these chariots of fire, these merkavim. I believe this is an Old Testament reference to what we would today call UFOs fighting on behalf of Israel."

This is an example of the Biblical UFO, the chariot of fire, seen in a military context, intended not to lead the Israelites through the desert or to take Elijah aloft, but to wage war in defense of the Israelites, who would otherwise have been hopelessly outnumbered and defeated.

THE UFO DEFENSE PHENOMENA

CONTINUES IN MODERN TIMES

In the modern era, Stearman said, particularly late 1947 through 1948, the vehicles of wonder were seen not only in the United States and Europe but throughout the Middle East. They were reported as disc-shaped and sometimes cigar-shaped. Sometimes they were suspected of being secret Russian weapons or invasions from another planet. But there exists a pattern wherein UFO sightings flaps were timed around crucial events in Israel.

"UFOs made their first really dramatic appearances," Stearman said, "in 1947 and 1948. That would be the Jewish year 5708, which corresponds to 47-48 in the Christian calendar. Of course, that was the time of the rebirth of Israel. These were years when great battles were being fought by human beings in Israel, but the idea is that perhaps someone else was taking notice of this on a higher plane.

"Just about ten years later, in early October of 1956," he contin-

THE ARK OF THE COVENANT AND OTHER SECRET WEAPONS OF THE ANCIENTS

A UFO photographed landing in Israel

ued, "during the great Sinai Campaign of Israel against Egypt, there were great numbers of sightings of UFOs. It was quite commonly reported in the newspapers of the Middle East, particularly the Israeli newspapers."

In the Jewish year 5727, timed with the late spring of 1967, the Six Day War between Israel and Egypt erupted, and again there was a great UFO flap throughout the world, according to Stearman. Frequent UFO sightings were also part of the Yom Kippur War against Israel in September and October of 1973. There was even a much earlier UFO wave in 1897, when the first Zionist Congress was held in Basel, Switzerland, to discuss the creation of a Jewish state in Palestine. At the time, the late 19th century, the unknown flying craft were called "airships" and were reported throughout the world, as recounted in various sources on the history of the UFO phenomenon.

FOR WHOM GOD FIGHTS

So just what are the UFO occupants trying to say about their relationship to Israel?

"The Bible speaks," Stearman replied, "of the fiery chariots being like heavenly ambassadors, or sometimes they're called heavenly messengers, or angels. You can call them beings from another dimension. They're commonly called aliens. But the prophets of ancient Israel said that these were the watchmen watching over Israel. They were acting on behalf of the people of Israel, according to the will of God. Now, that's what the Bible specifically says."

Does that mean the UFOs are making a show of force intended to let the world know they will protect Israel?

Stearman replied in the affirmative, saying, "Perhaps there is a battle, an ultra-dimensional battle – a battle behind the scenes – taking place between those who favor one side or the other. There's an earthly battle going on and there appears to be an ultra-dimensional battle going on, too. And it seems that every time Israel is threatened, the War in Heaven also seems to accelerate so that it becomes visible in this dimension as UFO and strange creature reports.

"The battle becomes pitched," he continued, "and becomes more visible to human eyes. In the Old Testament, one of the titles of the Lord is 'Lord of Hosts.' And that title essentially is a military title. It's like being General of the Heavenly Army. One of the major Bible themes is that the Lord fights on behalf of His people. In fact, one of the meanings of the name Israel is 'for whom God fights.' Each time Israel is in peril, these fiery chariots roll into action on behalf of Israel."

THE ARK OF THE COVENANT AND OTHER SECRET WEAPONS OF THE ANCIENTS

THE LORD AND HIS WEAPONS

A certain passage from the Book of Isaiah might be relevant to the discussion. Isaiah, Chapter 13, beginning with verse four, says, "Hark, a tumult on the mountains as of a great multitude, Hark, an uproar of kingdoms, of nations gathering together! The Lord of Hosts is mustering a host for battle.

"They come from a distant land, from the end of the heavens, the Lord and THE WEAPONS OF HIS INDIGNATION (emphasis mine), to destroy the whole earth,

"Wail, for the day of the Lord is near; as destruction from the Almighty it will come! Therefore, all hands will be feeble, and every man's heart will melt, and they will be dismayed. Pangs and agony will seize them; they will be in anguish like a woman in travail.

"They will look aghast at one another; their faces will be aflame. Behold, the day of the Lord comes, cruel, with wrath and fierce anger, to make the earth a desolation and to destroy its sinners from it."

We have here a most telling phrase, one that is more than relevant to the theme of ancient weaponry that runs throughout this book. When Isaiah refers to the "weapons of His indignation," no other specifics are given. Nevertheless, we are dealing with weapons of God's own design and implementation, presumably a matter of heavenly technology light years beyond anything man will have developed by the time the prophecy is fulfilled. The idea that mass destruction will be the end result of the Lord's unleashing of His weapons is a given, as He plainly states his intent to "make the earth a desolation" and to wipe out the sinners who have incurred his righteous wrath.

The weapons will clearly take mankind to the outer extremes of fear, of sheer terror, creating such agony that men's hearts will melt and they will be in a state of anguish comparable to a woman in labor. In other words, they will become so afraid that they will cease to be "men" at all. The Day of the Lord is even labeled as "cruel," the only such use of the term in relation to God that I know of in the Bible. The implication is that God will be punishing the cruelty of the earth in the same spirit as the "an eye for an eye" commandment from the books of Moses' law.

The instrument of God's wrath described in Isaiah is perhaps similar to the "Brahmastra" and "Brahmashira" weapons described in the chapter on the weaponry of ancient India elsewhere in this book. Both of those "messengers of death" were designed and controlled by the Hindu God of Creation, Brahma, without whose blessing and permission the weapons bearing his name could not be used. As with Jehovah's weapons of indignation, so are Brahma's decidedly his own, and are also intended to execute divine judgment on a massive scale when the time comes.

THE ARK OF THE COVENANT AND OTHER SECRET WEAPONS OF THE ANCIENTS

THE ARK OF THE COVENANT AND OTHER SECRET WEAPONS OF THE ANCIENTS

THE IRON THUNDERBOLT: TELLTALE SIGNS OF

KINETIC ENERGY WEAPONS IN ANCIENT BATTLES

By Olav Phillips

Warfare is as old as humanity, its devastation only limited by humanity's level of technological evolution and innovation. In Paleolithic times, humans fought with rocks; the Iron Age brought us swords and spears; and the information age has brought us cyber-warfare. New warfare types, all equally devastating, equally limited by technological innovation. As a civilization, humans strive towards a technical achievement, an achievement attained through warfare. We fight because it is who we are and it is who we have always been from the beginning of time.

That being said, what if, in a time before modern humanity, there was a cataclysmic war? A war fought between two opposing forces, members of a lost civilization whose technology rivaled modern humanity. Is it possible? According to ancient Hindu texts, it is not only possible but probable.

The cataclysmic war in question was described in great detail in an ancient text called the Mahabharata, believed to have been written some 12,000 years ago. It is commonly held to have described the events of a dynastic struggle for the throne of Hastinapura, ruled by the Kuru clan. According to the Mahabharata, the war was fought between two

THE ARK OF THE COVENANT AND OTHER SECRET WEAPONS OF THE ANCIENTS

sub-clans, the Kaurava and Pandava, ultimately culminating in a final battle called the "The Great Battle of Kurukshetra." The battle was ultimately won by the Pandavas, who inherited a land devastated by their own making.

It is that war, and the descriptions of various forms of high tech weaponry, which have long haunted archeologists. Descriptions of Vimana (aircraft), massive explosions and fireballs which would require an unimaginable level of technology.

THE ARK OF THE COVENANT AND OTHER SECRET WEAPONS OF THE ANCIENTS

Take this excerpt from the Mahabharata as an example:

"...a single projectile charged with all the power of the Universe. An incandescent column of smoke and flame, As bright as the thousand suns, Rose in all its splendor ... a perpendicular explosion with its billowing smoke clouds ... the cloud of smoke rising after its first explosion formed into expanding round circles like the opening of giant parasols ... it was an unknown weapon, an iron thunderbolt, a gigantic messenger of death, which reduced to ashes the entire race of the Vrishnis and the Andhakas. ...The corpses were so burned as to be unrecognizable. The hair and nails fell out; pottery broke without apparent cause and the birds turned white. After a few hours, all foodstuffs were infected ... to escape from this fire, the soldiers threw themselves in streams to wash themselves and their equipment."

This quote is often held to represent the explosion of a massive nuclear weapon or even multiple nuclear weapons, but what if the weapon used was not actually nuclear in nature? Is it possible that the ancient Rama soldiers possessed a weapon just as devastating as a

THE ARK OF THE COVENANT AND OTHER SECRET WEAPONS OF THE ANCIENTS

nuclear weapon but still not a nuclear weapon?

In the last few decades, ruins have started to emerge which show a high level of destruction including massive heat, blast waves and ash. Still, there seems there to be something missing if it was indeed a nuclear exchange. Such a large nuclear exchange would have engulfed the entire world, but what is missing in the archeological evidence is the larger environmental devastation which would have resulted from even a medium-sized nuclear battle.

The Red Cross estimates that a medium-sized nuclear exchange, with modern weaponry, the equivalent of some 100 Hiroshima-size nuclear devices, would produce over five million tons of radioactive soot that would enshroud the earth and cause the global temperature to fall by an average of 1.3C and result in the deaths of over one billion people due to starvation and sickness.

The outcome of even a "controlled" nuclear exchange has long been the crucible of modern military planners. Nuclear warfare is very much a situation in which a nation would win the war, maybe, but also lose the planet as it plunges into a darkened nuclear winter and massive amounts of the population die. This had lead modern humans to invest in new types of non-nuclear weapons which still provide a devastating impact on the enemy. From the neutron bomb to new types of chemical agents, all are designed to kill the enemy en masse but not destroy the environment long term.

Still we have the description, from the Mahabharata, of a large-scale conflict producing explosions, fireballs, shockwaves and other significant damage.

During the excavations of Harappa and Mohenjo-Daro, two locations believed to have been involved in this cataclysmic war, some interesting archeological evidence was found. At street level, archeologists discovered dozens of skeletons scattered about the cities, still

THE ARK OF THE COVENANT AND OTHER SECRET WEAPONS OF THE ANCIENTS

holding hands and cascaded through the streets as if some instant death had descended upon them. People were found lying, unburied, in the streets of the city. As excavations moved down along the street level, some 44 scattered skeletons in total were found, all having been seemingly flattened to the ground. In one stunning case, a father, mother and child were found flattened in the street, face down and still holding hands. Interestingly, there is no apparent cause of a physically violent death.

In Harappa and Mohenjo-Daro there was evidence of heavy radiation saturation in the ground, but this has been shown possibly to be due to modern environmental damage. Still, how can one explain such a cataclysmic death of two ancient cities? Their description is very much

THE ARK OF THE COVENANT AND OTHER SECRET WEAPONS OF THE ANCIENTS

like those of Pompeii and Herculaneum and what befell the inhabitants of those doomed Roman cities, destroyed during the eruption of Mt. Vesuvius.

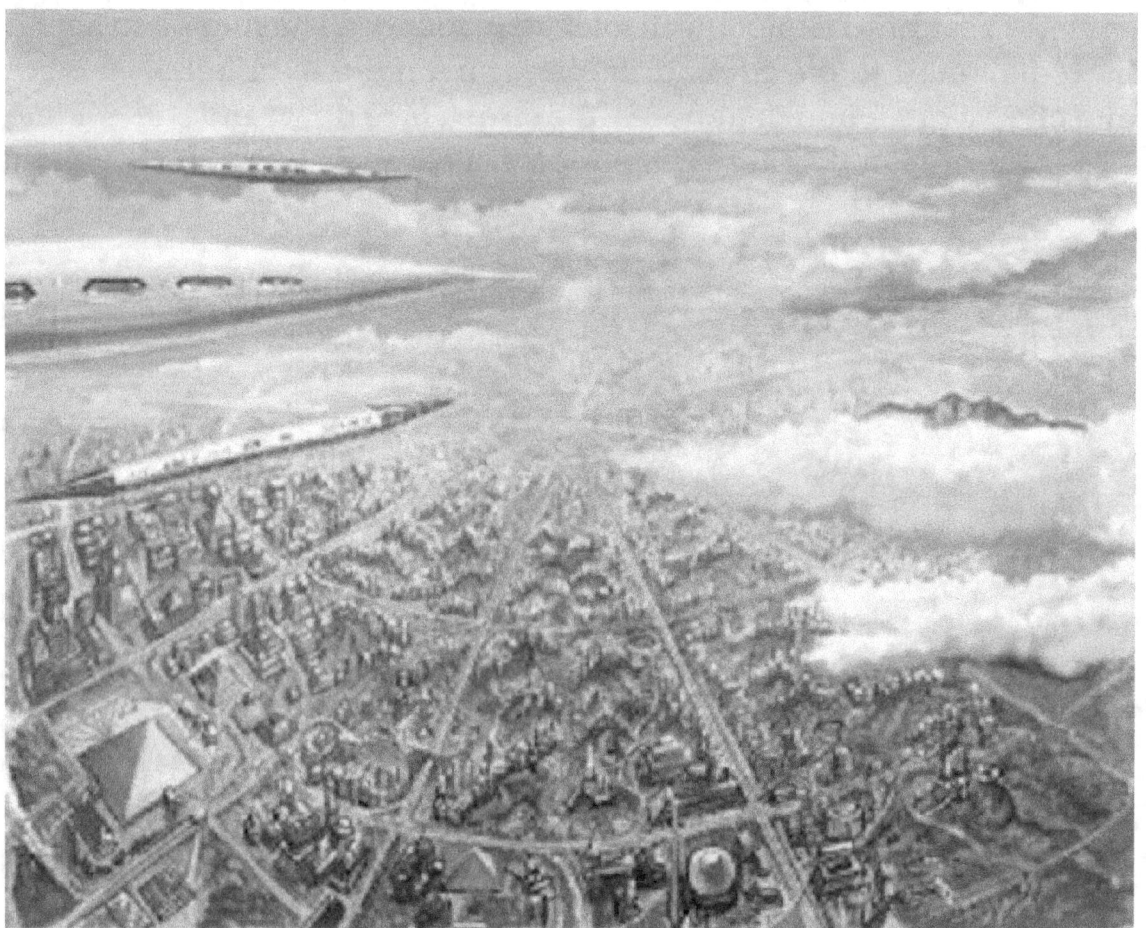

What's interesting is that Harappa and Mohenjo-Daro are not the only cities to have suffered such cataclysmic destruction. There are other cities, found throughout northern India, which appear to have suffered from explosions of massive magnitude. One such city, found in an area between the Ganges and the mountains of Rajmahal, appears to have been destroyed by intense heat. The walls and foundations of the ancient buildings are fused together and melted while other buildings show evidence of shockwave damage.

THE ARK OF THE COVENANT AND OTHER
SECRET WEAPONS OF THE ANCIENTS

There is also the question of anomalous craters such as the Lonar crater. The presence of these craters near some of these sites has led traditional archeologists to believe that the devastation found was caused by meteor impacts. But those same craters could indicate the use of kinetic bombardments.

Kinetic bombardment, or the use of super-dense chunks of material dropped at terminal velocity from orbit or high altitude, would produce an effect similar to a small-scale nuclear device, minus the radiation, unless the material was radioactive. Nevertheless, even if the material was radioactive, the radioactive contamination would be localized due to the nature of the device not exploding outwards.

THE ARK OF THE COVENANT AND OTHER SECRET WEAPONS OF THE ANCIENTS

What would be produced is an enormous fireball and a tremendous shockwave which would radiate outwards from the impact site. The superheated shockwave and concussive force wall would explain the collapse of structures and the scorching, but, more importantly, the craters. Kinetic weapons are also highly target-able since their firing angle can be computed from orbit. In fact, in modern times, much effort has been put into something called "Project Thor" or the "Rods from God," a system which hurls telephone pole-sized tungsten rods from orbit for the purpose of targeted, non-nuclear strikes.

This possible scenario is supported by the statement in the Mahabharata description of an "Iron Thunderbolt" which produced "an incandescent column of smoke and flame as bright as the thousand suns that rose in all its splendor." This seems to describe an object descending from orbit with a brilliant light, very much what you would see as a hypervelocity telephone pole-size rod, or something larger possibly, fell from the sky wrapped in a plasma sheath. The incandescence would have been brilliant, almost blinding.

There is also the reference to perpendicular smoke clouds rising up that would seem to indicate the possibility of several devices being used in the attack. A nuclear device would generate a single massive mushroom-shaped cloud, which would climb up into the atmosphere.

The concussive force of such an impact would shatter pottery, fell walls and, as I mentioned previously, the superheated shockwave would fuse rock as well as blow apart buildings.

Then there is the statement, "The entire race of the Vrishnis and the Andhakas ...The corpses were so burned as to be unrecognizable." This could very well have been due to the resulting superheated shockwave. What is harder to reconcile is statements such as "The hair and nails fell out; Pottery broke without apparent cause, and the birds turned white. After a few hours, all foodstuffs were infected ..." These statements would lead me to believe that the kinetic kill device may have been irradiated. Irradiating a device like that would produce localized radiation sickness much like a dirty bomb, but again, due to the style of delivery mechanism, the impact would have been localized.

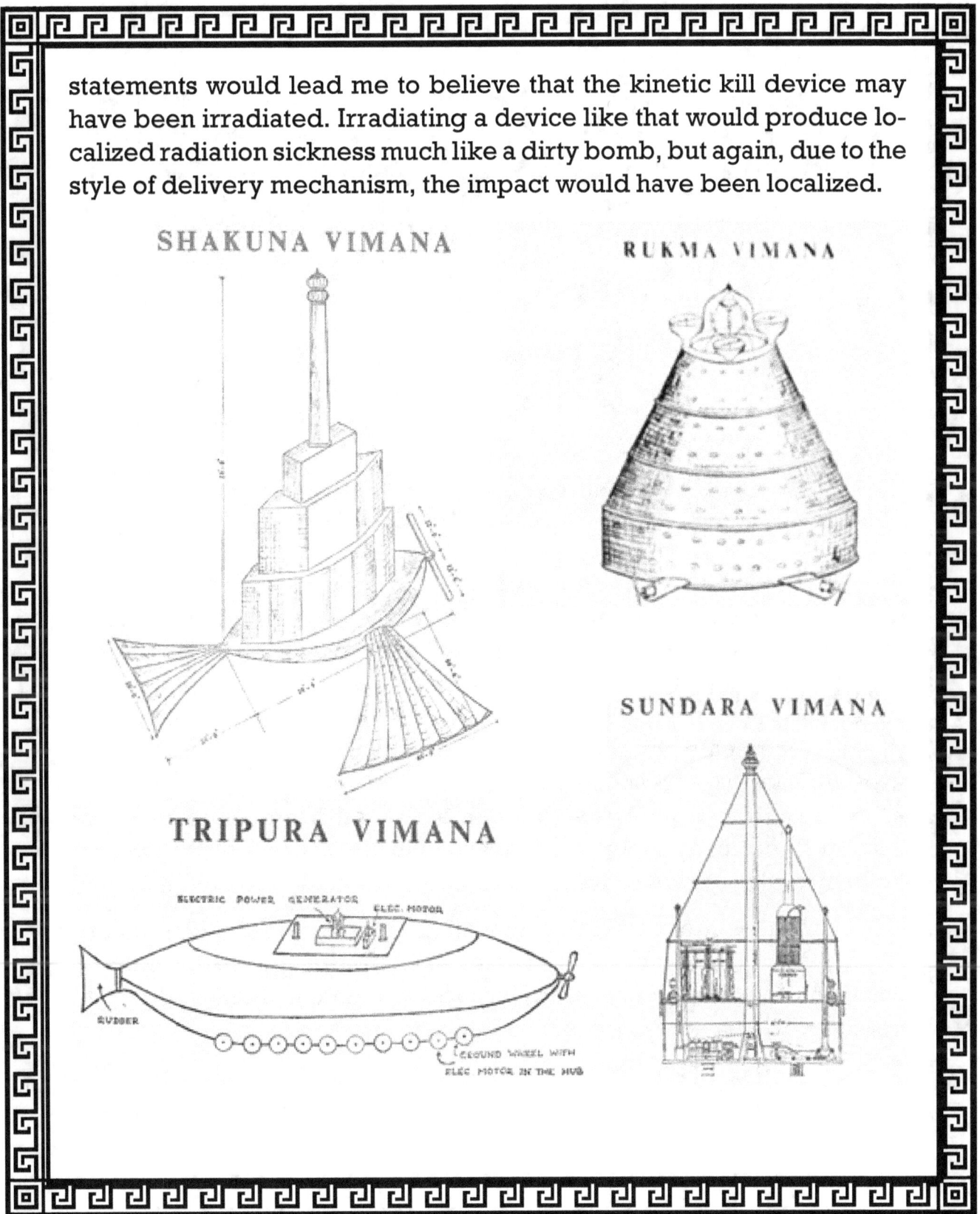

SHAKUNA VIMANA

RUKMA VIMANA

SUNDARA VIMANA

TRIPURA VIMANA

THE ARK OF THE COVENANT AND OTHER SECRET WEAPONS OF THE ANCIENTS

The use of such a weapon would also explain the presence of fused glass at these sites. Commonly called "Tektites," these glass globules are found around the immediate area, as well as in the general region, as ejecta is blown up into the atmosphere and away from the impact suite. The tektites are also found amongst large horizontal sheets of glass, which would again seem to indicate a powerful, but non-nuclear, fireball. Likewise, locations possessing tektites or glassy fields found at various areas from Africa to India, and even North America, were also probably hit by super-massive heat. But the lack of radioactive contamination on a grand scale is evidence of Kinetic Bombardment.

Kinetic Bombardment in modern times seems to be the path going forward. Since the 1950s, when RAND first proposed the idea of using super-dense kinetic energy weapons, military planners throughout the world have latched onto this idea.

In fact, in a 2003 USAF report, the US Air Force suggested that a 6.1 m 0.3 m tungsten cylinder impacting at Mach 10 has the equivalent

THE ARK OF THE COVENANT AND OTHER SECRET WEAPONS OF THE ANCIENTS

kinetic energy of 11.5 tons of TNT (or 7.2 tons of dynamite). So, as late as 2003, the US Air Force is still planning the use of such devices, not to mention the persistent rumors that Project Thor, as well as other SDI (Strategic Defense Initiative) hardware, was secretly placed into orbit in the 1980s under Ronald Reagan. The idea of "hypervelocity rod bundles" has even made its way into popular culture, having been used extensively in the movie "GI Joe: Retaliation."

It would stand to reason that, with the current level of technology humanity possesses, military planners have steered towards lethal weapons but also weapons which do not have a long lasting global impact. If we project this idea backwards, it would make sense that the participants in the Great War in the Mahabharata would have reached a similar point. Recognizing that a large-scale nuclear exchange would irrevocably destroy the very land they seek to possess, they too may have opted for a devastating weapon without long-term environmental damage.

Another telling quote from the ancient texts indicates that a large number of "arrow of flame" weapons seemed to descend in all directions. "The Earth shook, scorched by the terrible heat of this weapon. Elephants burst into flames and ran to and fro in a frenzy, seeking a

THE ARK OF THE COVENANT AND OTHER SECRET WEAPONS OF THE ANCIENTS

protection from terror. Over a vast area other animals crumpled to the ground and died. The waters boiled, and the creatures residing therein also died. From all points of the compass the arrows of the flame rained continuously!"

This, too, would support the use of kinetic energy rods or "arrows of flame" since their descent would very much resemble a falling, flaming arrow with stabilizer fins and a control pod. If the Mahabharata is to be believed, the Rama certainly possessed the needed technology to develop such a weapon system. Through the use of the Vimana they also possessed the technical skills to place these devices into orbit and fire them accurately against both military and non-military targets much the same way Allied bombers targeted Dresden in Germany for firebombing to create destabilization in the populace.

The deployment of kinetic weaponry also seems to fit this idea that there are locations scattered around the Earth which show signs of catastrophic devastation of cities from around the same point, but at the same time lack the long-term radiation damaged caused by nuclear weapons. If there were an ancient high-tech civilization of this magnitude, it would be possible to surmise that that civilization possessed colonies in other geographies. Those colonies would also have been subject to attack, and to that end researchers have found heat-fused walls, tektites, and evidence of shockwave damage. It's also important to point out that these settlements appear to have been destroyed at around the same time period of 10,000 years ago. This includes the legendary Gobekli Tepe archeological site, which shows evidence of flash scorching, shockwave damage, fused ground glass and a boundary layer of ash.

At Gobekli Tepe, this boundary layer, extreme heat and concussive damage have led conventional archeology to conclude that Gobekli Tepe was destroyed by a meteor. A hypothesis, which, if hypervelocity rod bundles destroyed Gobekli Tepe, would be fundamentally correct

THE ARK OF THE COVENANT AND OTHER SECRET WEAPONS OF THE ANCIENTS

since the damage, would be similar.

If these sites were destroyed by kinetic bombardment from orbit, wouldn't there still be evidence in space? The short answer is "Possibly." This would depend on the level of sophistication of the launch platform since, without constant maintenance, the weapons platforms would orbitally degrade over time and would plunge into the atmosphere to be burned up. There is, however, an anomalous satellite which might actually be a surviving weapons platform.

Called the "Black Knight," it first came into the public realm in 1957 when a mysterious satellite shadowed Sputnik for several hours before disappearing. At that time we lacked the technology to truly investigate the satellite and the government seemed to come up with a plausible story. Then it came back in 1960.

The story was even reported by the famous Fortean writer John Keel in "Disneyland of the Gods." Keel related that in February 1960 the US detected an unknown object apparently in polar orbit over the Earth. At that time, this was a shocking feat that neither the United States nor Soviets had been able to duplicate. The mys-

THE ARK OF THE COVENANT AND OTHER SECRET WEAPONS OF THE ANCIENTS

tery deepened when it was revealed that the object was several orders of magnitude larger than anything either country would have been able to launch into orbit. The same story was also discussed in the March 7th, 1960, issue of "Time Magazine." In an article titled "Science: Space Watch's First Catch," "Time" informed readers that a mysterious satellite had set off a defense network called "Dark Fence" and appeared to take up stationary orbit over the North Pole. Again, the United States Air Force was at a loss as to the origin of the device, finally saying it was a space derelict from a previous attempted launch.

The dark "Knight" has also been linked to a mysterious satellite which lived at the L5 space point and was beaming back messages called Long Delay Echoes, or LDE's, which date back to an anomalous event in 1927 when ham operators beamed signals to a specific quadrant of space only to have their messages beamed back at increasing intervals. In the 1970s, Duncan Lunan, an amateur astronomer from Scotland, claimed to have decoded the message but later revised his decoding. Still, it is an object of great antiquity, appears to have an intelligent control system and has been known to move as well as change frequency to avoid jamming.

The "Black Knight" could very well be the launch platform for the ancient attacks at Harappa and Mohenjo-Daro as well as the numerous other sites which may have been involved in the conflagration. It would make sense, considering the satellite has been seen to adjust its orbit autonomously. This would have allowed the platform to move as required to bombard targets at any location. It also makes sense if it is the last of its constellation. Having expended its munitions, the "Black Knight" stands still, vigilantly monitoring its targets as well as investigating new objects in its proximity. The other satellites would long ago have failed, fallen back to Earth and burned up, or perhaps debris from an orbital battle would have degraded and reentered as well, destroying all the evidence.

THE ARK OF THE COVENANT AND OTHER SECRET WEAPONS OF THE ANCIENTS

Another element of this story, which supports the "Black Knight" as a surviving orbital bombardment platform, is the Long Delay Echoes or LDE's. The LDE's that have been detected may have been part of the command and control system for the space based weaponry.

So what do we really know? We have a historical chronicle of a massive war. That war was a technological war with aircraft (vimanas), massive loss of life, enigmatic craters and decimated cities, all recounted in very vivid descriptions. Those descriptions seem to talk about cylinders, be they iron thunderbolts or flaming arrows, which were superheated, flaming, falling and extremely bright. We also see an outcome lacking global ecological collapse and long-term ecological damage through nuclear fallout. When coupled with modern research into kinetic energy weapons intended to preserve the lands one seeks to conquer rather than reducing them to radioactive wastelands, there seems to be compelling evidence that an alternative, and very advanced, weapon system was utilized in a catastrophic ancient war.

About Olav Phillips

Olav Phillips is a Conspiracy Researcher who specializes in the Secret Space Program, Exotic Aircraft, High Technology, Foreign Policy, Pre-History and Mysterious Civilizations. He is a regular contributor to "Paranoia Magazine" and "ConspiracyHQ." He has also written for "Mysteries Magazine" and served as Executive Producer and Principle Researcher for Ground Zero Radio with Clyde Lewis (Nationally Syndicated by Premiere Radio Networks). Olav has also appeared on many popular radio shows and television presentations such as: The Outer Edge, The Higher Side Chats, ConspiracyHQ TV, Shadows In The Dark Radio, Coast to Coast AM, Voyager (RAI Due), as well as being a long-time contributor to Ground Zero Radio's investigations, including the famous Tracy, CA, UFO Crash case featured on "UFO Hunters." Olav has also contributed to many of the television presentations you've seen on Area 51, UFOs and conspiracies.

THE ARK OF THE COVENANT AND OTHER SECRET WEAPONS OF THE ANCIENTS

Olav is the owner of The Anomalies Channel, an online video channel with over 26,000 subscribers and hundreds of videos available to ROKU players all over the world as well as The Anomalies Network, which is the primary source for his writings and research.

http://www.anomalies.net/wp-content/uploads/2014/03/olavPhillips.png

THE ARK OF THE COVENANT AND OTHER SECRET WEAPONS OF THE ANCIENTS

EXTENSIVE EVIDENCE OF PRE-HISTORIC NUCLEAR WAR

By Brad Steiger

"Then the Lord rained down fire and tar from heaven upon Sodom and Gomorrah, and utterly destroyed them...." —Genesis 19:24.

THE "FUSED GREEN GLASS" CONTROVERSY

I remain open to many theories of Earth's prehistory. While patches of "fused green glass" may in certain instances have been caused by air blasts from meteors, as some experts have claimed, I wonder if such a natural phenomenon could have created all twenty-eight fields of blackened and shattered stones that cover as many as 7000 miles each in western Arabia. The stones are densely grouped, as if they might be the remains of cities, sharp-edged, and burned black. Other authorities have decreed that they are not volcanic in origin, but appear to date from the period when Arabia was thought to be a lush and fruitful land that suddenly became scorched into an instant desert.

What we know today as the Sahara Desert was once a tropical region of heavy vegetation, abundant rainfall, and several large rivers. Scientists have discovered areas of the desert in which soils which once knew the cultivated influence of plow and farmer are now covered by a thin layer of sand. Researchers have also found an enormous reservoir of water below the parched desert area. The source of such a large deposit of water could only have been the heavy rains from the period

THE ARK OF THE COVENANT AND OTHER SECRET WEAPONS OF THE ANCIENTS

of time before a fiery devastation consumed the lush vegetation of the area.

On December 25, 2007, it was confirmed by a French scientist that excavations at the area of Khamis Bani Sa'ad in the Tehema district of the Hodeidah province have yielded over a thousand rare archaeological pieces dating back to 300,000 B.C.E. Before a dramatic climate change, the inhabitants at that time had been fishermen and had domesticated a number of animals no longer found in the region, including a species of horse currently found only in Middle Asia.

The Red Chinese have conducted atomic tests near Lob Nor Lake in the Gobi Desert, which have left large patches of the area covered with vitreous sand. But the Gobi has a number of other areas of glassy sand which have been known for thousands of years.

THE ARK OF THE COVENANT AND OTHER SECRET WEAPONS OF THE ANCIENTS

ANCIENT SANDS AND NEW MEXICO'S WHITE SANDS

Albion W. Hart, one of the first engineers to graduate from Massachusetts Institute of Technology, was assigned a project in the interior of Africa. While he and his men were traveling to an almost inaccessible region, they had first to cross a great expanse of desert. At the time, he was puzzled and quite unable to explain a large area of greenish glass which covered the sands as far as he could see.

"Later on during his life," wrote **Margarethe Casson** in *Rocks and Minerals* (No. 396, 1972), "he passed by the White Sands area after the first atomic explosion there and he recognized the same type of silica fusion which he had seen fifty years earlier in the African desert."

In 1947, in the Euphrates Valley of southern Iraq, where certain traditions place the Garden of Eden and where the ancient inhabitants of Sumer encountered the man-god Ea, exploratory digging unearthed a layer of fused, green glass. Archaeologists could not restrain themselves from noting the resemblance that the several-thousand-year-old fused glass bore to the desert floor at White Sands, New Mexico, after the first nuclear blasts in modem times had melted sand and rock.

In the United States, the Mohave Desert has large circular or polygonal areas that are coated with a hard substance very much like opaque glass.

While exploring Death Valley in 1850, **William Walker** claimed to have come upon the ruins of an ancient city. An end of the large building within the rubble had had its stones melted and vitrified.

Walker went on to state that the entire region between the Gila and St. John rivers was spotted with ruins. In each of the ancient settlements he had found evidence that they had been burned out by fire intense enough to have liquefied rock. Paving blocks and stone houses had been split with huge cracks, as if seared by some gigantic cleaver of fire.

THE ARK OF THE COVENANT AND OTHER SECRET WEAPONS OF THE ANCIENTS

SIMILAR PHENOMENA IN EUROPE AND TURKEY

Perhaps even more than the large areas of fused green glass, I am intrigued by the evidence of vitrified cities and forts, such as those discovered by Walker.

There are ancient hill forts and towers in Scotland, Ireland, and England in which the stoneworks have become calcined because of the great heat that had been applied. There is no way that lightning could have caused such effects.

Other hill forts from the Lofoten Islands off northern Norway to the Canary Islands off northwest Africa have become "fused forts." Erich A. von Fange comments that the "piled boulders of their circular walls have been turned to glass... by some intense heat."

THE ARK OF THE COVENANT AND OTHER SECRET WEAPONS OF THE ANCIENTS

Catal Huyukin, in north-central Turkey, thought to be one of the oldest cities in the world, appears, according to archaeological evidence, to have been fully civilized and then, suddenly, to have died out. Archaeologists were astonished to find thick layers of burned brick at one of the levels, called VIa. The blocks had been fused together by such intense heat that the effects had penetrated to a depth more than a meter below the level of the floors, where it carbonized the earth, the skeletal remains of the dead, and the burial gifts that had been interred with them. All bacterial decay had been halted by the tremendous heat.

THE ARK OF THE COVENANT AND OTHER SECRET WEAPONS OF THE ANCIENTS

When a large ziggurat in Babylonia was excavated, it presented the appearance of having been struck by a terrible fire that had split it down to its foundation. In other parts of the ruins, large sections of brickwork had been scorched into a vitrified state. Several masses of brickwork had been rendered into a completely molten state. Even large boulders found near the ruins had been vitrified.

The royal buildings at the north Syrian site known as Alalakh or Atchana had been so completely burned that the very core of the thick walls were filled with bright red, crumbling mud-bricks. The mud and lime wall plaster had been vitrified, and basalt wall slabs had, in some areas, actually melted.

THE NUKED RUINS OF OTHER CITIES

Between India's Ganges River and the Rajmahal Hills are scorched ruins which contain large masses of stone that have been fused and hollowed. Certain travelers who have ventured to the heart of the Indian forests have reported ruins of cities in which the walls have become huge slabs of crystal, due to some intense heat.

The ruins of the Seven Cities, located near the equator in the Province of Piaui, Brazil, appear to be the scene of a monstrous chaos. Since no geological explanation has yet been construed to fit the evidence before the archaeologists, certain of those who have investigated the site have said that the manner in which the stones have been dried out, destroyed and melted provokes images of Sodom and Gomorrah.

French researchers discovered the evidence of prehistoric spontaneous nuclear reaction at the Oklo mine, Pierrelatte, in Gabon, Africa. Scientists found that the ore of this mine contained abnormally low proportions of U235 such as found only in depleted uranium fuel taken from atomic reactors. According to those who examined the mine, the ore also contained four rare elements in forms similar to those found in depleted uranium.

THE ARK OF THE COVENANT AND OTHER SECRET WEAPONS OF THE ANCIENTS

Although the modern world did not experience atomic power until the 1940s, there is an astonishing amount of evidence that nuclear effects may have occurred in prehistoric times, leaving behind sand melted into glass in certain desert areas, hill forts with vitrified portions of stone walls, and the remains of ancient cities that had been destroyed by what appeared to have been extreme heat – far beyond that which could have been scorched by the torches of primitive armies. In each instance, the trained and experienced archaeologists who encountered such anomalous finds have stressed the point that none of these catastrophes had been caused by volcanoes, by lightning, by crashing comets, or by conflagrations set by humankind.

THE ARK OF THE COVENANT AND OTHER SECRET WEAPONS OF THE ANCIENTS

THE ARK OF THE COVENANT AND OTHER SECRET WEAPONS OF THE ANCIENTS

FOR THE GLORY OF THE GODS

By Timothy Green Beckley

Even though we think of ourselves as living in a civilized society (do we really?), man has always seen fit to dedicate himself to engaging in bloody combat, be it hand to hand or by weapons of mass destruction. There doesn't seem to be a time in history when he hasn't picked up the sword to do battle with a perceived – or all too real – foe. Either to protect himself, his family, his kingdom, or to spread his faith.

But when a true warrior goes into battle, he must protect himself at all costs. Camouflage to hide from his enemy in the brush. Chain armament to cover the most sensitive parts of his body for when the enemy comes at him dead on. Or a shield made of the strongest metal possible so that it cannot be easily penetrated by any deadly projectile be it arrow or sword or spear.

If one has to die for heath, heartland or because of a sense of religious fervor, one should go to Valhalla with their boots on and their weapons fully "charged" and "sharpened" and clutched in their mighty hands (just like NRA spokesperson Charles Heston imagined doing while clasping a semi-automatic rifle in his hand). A mighty warrior has to go down swinging, and that means you need more than the guts for glory – you need a powerful saber or some device which will knock the enemies' socks off (or do far worse, if truth be told).

THE ARK OF THE COVENANT AND OTHER SECRET WEAPONS OF THE ANCIENTS

Now there is only so much damage the ancients could have done with the weapons of the day. After all, you can only jettison a spear once and then you are caught empty handed and thus closer to the grave. A bow and arrow might be a little better for distance, but, as you forge ahead against a well-fortified army hiding behind a castle wall, you are right out in the open. So you had better get your act together – and quite quickly or you will go down in a flash – and no telling what lies at the bottom of that boggy moat.

So what to do? Well, you can either desert the ranks (and probably be beheaded if caught) or you can call upon the "powers that be" (who you are probably offering your soul to anyway) for guidance and support (i.e. firepower). And, if you are lucky and the gods (extraterrestrials?) hear your cry, they might provide you with a weapon that will blow the enemy out of the water or turn them into a pillar or salt (sound familiar?).

TRIUMPH OF THE IMMORTALS

Going back to when time began, humankind seems to have had an accord with "The Other," a term minted by prolific author Brad Steiger to apply to the intercession of "aliens" in our social structure worldwide. Such visits by Ultra-terrestrials have been popularized by the likes of ancient astronaut theorists such as Erich Von Daniken, Brinsley Le Poer Trench and W. R. Drake. The History2 Channel series "Ancient Aliens" has been a persistent hit, airing for over six seasons and showing no decrease in popularity.

Some of the most devastating – and well-documented – weapons found in reports that predate the birth of Christ deal with the use of laser and nuclear-like arms fired primarily from the sky which can be found throughout Sanskrit writings as well as other ancient text. Contributors Sean Casteel and Olav Phillips cover what has been called "the power of creation" very thoroughly. Known most often as the

THE ARK OF THE COVENANT AND OTHER SECRET WEAPONS OF THE ANCIENTS

"Brahmastra," it was a dreadful instrument that could immobilize any number of combatants, stalling their forward movements.

Those that were outside the range of this devastating force said the effect on the fallen was always catastrophic and almost always the same – first their faces became gaunt, than ash white as they became frozen for all eternity. Immobilized, they stood rigid then eventually crumbled to the ground. It was like they had been felled by a current that passed through the ground then shot up their spine. Sephiroth, a senior member of a Hindu group, advances the theory that the Naga Ashtra "is a 'snake'-like force which slithers down to its victim, striking the most vulnerable spot, and kills if not paralyzes its victim." I've also seen reference to the fact that it turned these seasoned warriors' flesh blue. One faithful devotee of the Hindu faith named Yogkriya insists that, "Only a couple of people present on the earth today have the knowledge of a few of these weapons. A yogi from Siddhashram a few years ago set a fire in an area in a forest. Such a fire is different from the ordinary fire and cannot be ordinarily extinguished by water. He then used vayu astra to extinguish it."

Legend tells us that the gods who resided upon Mount Olympus could have been seated at the control panel of a mighty particle beam weapons system that might easily rival today's star wars technology. If they wanted to befriend an individual or an entire army, they could provide them with the ultimate thunderclap of doom. If, on the other hand, they had some reason to despise you, well, all hell (Hades) was sure to break out across the front lines.

GREEK SWORDS OF MYTHOLOGY

"The Grecians of bygone times – as well as some of those still living in the shadow of Olympus – believe that their lives are intertwined with the existence of the gods. Their wars and battles are but a reflection of the greater battles fought in the court of Zeus," notes and website

THE ARK OF THE COVENANT AND OTHER SECRET WEAPONS OF THE ANCIENTS

called "2 Clicks Guide to Swords." The author of the guide explains that it is "not surprising that (magical) Greek god swords exist, at least in oral tradition and myths. The swords of Greek gods have magical, healing, and superhuman powers. There are instances where they give their swords to humans especially during a time of peril or when a mortal is fighting against a deity. For example, Perseus was given one of the Greek god's swords to kill the monster Medusa, a monster with a hair of snakes and whose scales were invincible to human-made weapons. It is not only in myths that the gods intervened in the affairs of mortals. The kings, or the rulers, of the city-states sometimes received the swords of the Greek gods. King Peleus, the father of Trojan war hero Achilles, was given a sword made by Hephaestus, the god of metalworking."

There are dozens of legendary artifacts that are said to possess supernatural powers.

Here are some of the formidable weapons the Olympian immortals ably wielded:

Poseidon's and

Neptune's Trident:

Striking the trident on the ground could cause the earth to tremble and shake for miles, opening up huge fissures that could swallow up those who dared challenge the divinity. The three-headed spear of Neptune could also create huge tidal waves and storms at sea.

Apollo's Bow and Arrow: A mere lancing of the flesh could be devastating, causing a stroke that could

THE ARK OF THE COVENANT AND OTHER SECRET WEAPONS OF THE ANCIENTS

put those stricken into an eternal sleep. Believed to also spread famine and cause unspeakable health problems to all those thus pierced.

The Argo: A mighty warship which had a life of its own and could move swiftly through the seas, eradicating all its enemies if under siege. The ship was made of impenetrable oak timber from the sacred forest of Dodona, where a famous oracle resided. The ship was said to be able to speak, giving victorious decrees to its crew. It also had large mirrors mounted toward the bow which, when aimed at a challenger to the rule of the high seas, would come close to incinerating the enemy.

Sun Chariot: First portrayed in stories of Helios and then Apollo, the Chariot of the Sun could stream across the sky, sending down immense heat waves in the form of lightning or burning spears and decimating those in the chariot's path.

Pandora's Box: Envelopes anyone who opens the box (actually a giant vase or jar) in a deadly "shadow," thus unleashing all the evils of the world upon them.

Helm (Helmet) of Hades: Anyone wearing this helmet becomes invisible, and we know that there are no limits to what an invisible person or entity can do to overcome obstacles.

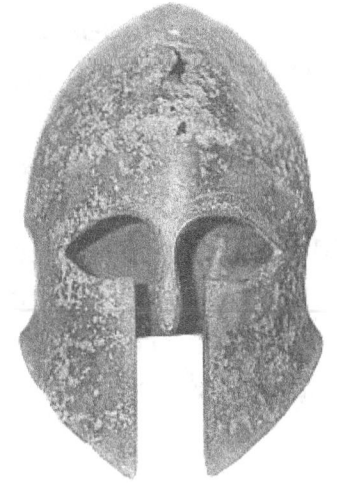

Sickle of Cronus (Saturn): We best recognize him today as "Father Time" and we know the old boy has a reputation for cutting people down in their old age (or youth, if you get on his wrong side!). There was no escaping from this god, as Cronus' sickle, which had the strength of a diamond in luster, could wreak hell through anything, including the most impenetrable of armament.

THE ARK OF THE COVENANT AND OTHER SECRET WEAPONS OF THE ANCIENTS

Sword of Death: Greek Mythology has it that if the bearer of this sinister implement of terror so much as possesses a lock of your hair or a nail clipping you are condemned to die an agonizing death if they so wish it.

ADVANCED WEAPONS OF ANTIQUITY

Shaman and expert on antiquities Dr. Maria D' Andrea unequivocally believes that in almost every culture there are those who are able to act as a go-between when it comes to communicating and receiving assistance from the gods. The host of a public access TV show on Long Island and author of numerous metaphysically oriented books, the Hungarian-born mystic has spent a lifetime flipping through the pages of history, collecting and deciphering the various texts which indicate that, "the gods are as real as you and I though, not in the physical sense. They come to us from a parallel universe. They may be deities, elementals and what we would call spirits, but they have the ability to direct our lives, guide our thinking, and even control the destiny of entire nations."

Though their agendas may not be apparent to us, and can be cleverly disguised, they often seem at the forefront when it comes to matters of war and global intrigue. "For are not the majority of battlefield skirmishes due primarily to differences in religion? How many millions have gone to their death because a 'voice' instructed them to pick up arms and fight for the glory of some unseen divinity?" Maria notes that in days of old magic played a great part in the forging of weapons. "The blacksmiths – the sword-smiths – often wore priestly robes while they heated and plied the best metals available to make their implements of destruction. They even chanted and said prayers over their furnaces as they shaped the iron and later the best grades of steel. Some of the highest quality swords were made from meteorites which, given that they fell from the heavens, certainly meant that they had to be powered by the lords of the universe." Anyone who did not take the task of the

THE ARK OF THE COVENANT AND OTHER SECRET WEAPONS OF THE ANCIENTS

village blacksmith seriously or who dared to gaze into his eyes found themselves likely to be exiled from the community at best, and put to death at the extreme. It has been said that as few as ten men could sometimes wipe out the conquering hordes if their weaponry had been blessed from 'above.'"

EXACTLY WHAT MAKES A WEAPON MAGICAL?

< Zeus and the Thunderbolt

Maria quotes an anonymous aficionado whose online handle is "Real World," regarding such matters: "We are told that the materials that the weapons are made out of have great relevance. Such materials in their natural state have affinity with the divine, so objects made from them are themselves sacred. As an example, Keris blades of the Indonesian archipelago islands made from meteorite iron thought to have been thrown to earth by the gods.

Likewise, the method of production is quite germane. "The forging process for bladed weapons is alchemical in itself, consisting of the transmutation of essential elements. When it comes to forging Japanese katana blades, numerous invocations are made to Shinto deities. Not to be dismissed out of hand are the decorations or application of spiritually significant artwork. This is very common throughout history with everything from full figural artwork such as the Keris hilts (carved sword handles made from heavy woods often with dramatic demonic figures) from Bali to talismanic workings, such as the Beduh magic squares on Middle Eastern swords, to prayers and religious inscriptions on the

THE ARK OF THE COVENANT AND OTHER SECRET WEAPONS OF THE ANCIENTS

swords of Christians going into battle." Furthermore, some weapons are said to literally be "possessed," the spirits or entities residing in the weapons themselves, such as in the case of the Hantu in keris swords.

KING ARTHUR'S EXCALIBUR

AND JOAN OF ARC'S FABELED SWORD

Arthur >

One of the best known examples of a "magical sword" would be the Sword of Excalibur, which united all of Great Britain behind King Arthur.

Historical scribe Roger Lancelyn Green, who breathed life into the many heroes of the Arthurian legends, tells how baby Arthur was left in the care of the wizard Merlin "in the Land of Mystery, Avalon. There the baby received three gifts from the powers of mystery: he would be the best of all knights, he would live long, and he would be the greatest king his land would ever know. Merlin then gave Arthur into the care of a good knight, Sir Ector, to be raised as his own son. So Arthur grew up, not knowing whose son he was, nor what his destiny would be."

Years later Merlin was riding through the forest with Arthur, who was sadden by the fact that he had lost his favorite sword, but he was instructed by the wizard not to be troubled because another, more powerful, sword awaited him that had been created in Avalon by fairy craft. Merlin told his protégé to "go down and speak with the Lady of the

THE ARK OF THE COVENANT AND OTHER SECRET WEAPONS OF THE ANCIENTS

Lake."

Doing so, Arthur took a "steep path to the side of the magic lake. Standing on the shore, he looked out across the quiet blue water – and there in the very centre of the lake he saw an arm clothed in white samite with a hand holding above the surface a wondrous sword with a golden hilt set with jewels, and a jeweled scabbard and belt."

At this juncture in the tale of the Lady of the Lake, "a beautiful damsel dressed in pale blue silk with a golden girdle" walks across the water until she stands before Arthur on the shore. The Lady asks Arthur if he wishes to "take the sword and wear it at your side?" Excalibur proves to be the witching sword of all time in that it unites the kingdom and turns Arthur into the most significant ruler Briton is ever to see. As to its magical powers, when Excalibur was first drawn, Arthur's enemies were blinded by its blade, which was as bright as thirty torches. Excalibur's scabbard was said to have powers of its own. Injuries from losses of blood, for example, would not kill the bearer. In some renderings, wounds received by one wearing the scabbard did not bleed at all. Excalibur cannot be used for an evil act or it will break. If someone holds it, they cannot lie. It can heal wounds and it inspires courage in all men who find themselves following in his path.

Unbeknownst to many there are other "weapons of wonderment" associated with King Arthur and the Knights of the Round Table. There is **Carnwennan,** which was a one-of-a-kind dagger which, when carried by a Knight of Arthur's choosing, would shroud them in utter darkness. Then there was **Caliburn**, a sword that shone as bright as thirty suns, and **Rhongomiant**, Arthur's personal holy lance, which provided instant justice to anyone who was "less than pure of heart."

"The second most highly appraised sword in the chronicles of Europe without a doubt belonged to Joan of Arc and was found concealed beneath the alter at Saint Catherine de Fierbois, where her voices

THE ARK OF THE COVENANT AND OTHER SECRET WEAPONS OF THE ANCIENTS

told her it would be located," D' Andrea said. "When she was brought to trial before being burned at the stake, her inquisitors wanted to know all manner of information about the sword. They wanted to know who forged it, and she told them it had been the archangel Saint Michael. At first the sword was full of rust, but then the rust fell away and there were five stars that seemingly indicated that the weapon had been sent from Heavenly realms." From all accounts, Joan battled feverishly with this blade, bringing the enemy to its knees and putting King Charles VII onto the throne of France.

THE SUPER WEAPONERY OF THE SAMURAI
AND THE VIKINGS

There are many other steels that have been associated with the wrath of the gods. They all did such massive damage to the keep the enemy at bay that they deserve more than a mere passing glance of a red hot lance.

In particular, the Japanese swords and the swords of the legendary Vikings are worthy of consideration in our tales of "super weaponry" from the pages of antiquity.

"One sword from the warrior culture of ancient Japan," D' Andrea informs us, "is known as the *Kusanagi-no-Tsurugi*, which was particularly useful when it came to fighting off hideous monsters to save in particular one wealthy land-owning family whose seven daughters had

THE ARK OF THE COVENANT AND OTHER SECRET WEAPONS OF THE ANCIENTS

been eaten by serpents. Likewise, the legend of the Samurai tells us that the Emperor was both mentally and physically stricken because many of his warriors were returning from the battlefields with damaged swords which had been snapped in two or otherwise impaired. A father and son blacksmith who most everyone believed possessed supernatural abilities were disgraced because their magic was not as powerful as thought. It was only after they had a dream in which the formula was given to them for a perfect blade – complete with the vision of a gleaming weapon – that honor was restored upon the troops returning from the next skirmish victorious.

"There is much in the way of ancient wisdom that is still protected and guarded. The Samurai sword-smiths were said to meditate intensely on their blades as they were being forged from the best metals. The process of how they got the blades so sharp is still a carefully kept secret." D'Andrea says that many of the blade-makers were in contact with divine sources which inspired them. "They would seek out the high-

THE ARK OF THE COVENANT AND OTHER
SECRET WEAPONS OF THE ANCIENTS

est mountains in order to receive telepathic communications. Some would go into a trace which would enable them to perfect their craft to a remarkable degree. They themselves became an energy source for transmissions from the gods. In turn, they injected this energy into their magical creation with every thrust of their hand tool. They were supposedly in contact with the ancient gods known as the Kami, who made sure the swords underwent an intense purification process which included bathing them in scented waters while chanting the exact words necessary to perform their task."

D'Andrea continues by recapping some of the supernaturally-inspired Norse weapons that enabled the Vikings to rout their opponents far and wide, throughout many lands.

"The legends of the Norse tell us that King Hogni's sword, identified as **Dainsleif**, came into play when he tried to pay off the father of a man whose daughter he had killed. When the father said no compensation would do, Hogni reportedly replied: 'Thou hast made this offer overlate, if thou wouldst make peace: for now I have drawn Dáinsleif, which the dwarves made, and which must cause a man's death every time it is bared, nor ever fails in its stroke; moreover, the wound heals not if one be scratched with it.'"

Odin & Frigga >

D'Andrea tells us that no review of Viking history would be

THE ARK OF THE COVENANT AND OTHER SECRET WEAPONS OF THE ANCIENTS

complete without at least a mention of **Odin's spear** and the **hammer of Thor.** "Odin's spear, **Gungnir**, never misses its mark and is composed of a rare sacred ash known as Yggdrasils, which can only be found at one particular location that is guarded by elves. Likewise, Thor's thunderous hammer, **Mjolnir**, has been depicted in movies, comics and in other portrayals of the famed Norse God. The hammer is so thunderous that it can level mountainous terrain into powder. One can only guess as to what voltage would have to be created for the God of Thunder and Lightning to alter the structure of such formerly great land masses."

JERICHO AND OTHER ANCIENT MEMORIES

Keeping us on track, the mystical and magical Ms. D' Andrea informs us that the tools of power utilized by the wizards of olden days came in various forms. "The heavens would open and the divine power would strike them. Maybe it was unseen; perhaps it was a beam from an extraterrestrial space ship sent from the gods who resided light years away. This energy that struck them cut across all barriers of time and space. If the aim of the gods is true, nothing can prevent them from sharing their powers with mortal collaborators.

"Symbols and colors, varying degrees of hot and cold, as well as the use of sound, added to the vitality and potency of the transmissions between humans and their source of 'inspiration.' We are told in the Bible that the walls of Jericho came tumbling down after the Israelite army marched around the city blowing their trumpets. There are some that think that sound and frequency played an important role in ancient cultures, including in the building of the pyramids of Egypt." Though we could tell the entire story of the fall of Jericho, associate Tim Swartz has set that as one of his tasks in an accompanying chapter, so we will silence the earth shattering sounds of the triumphs of the Israelites for the time being.

We could venture forth and tell of many miracle weapons of great

THE ARK OF THE COVENANT AND OTHER SECRET WEAPONS OF THE ANCIENTS

marauding qualities.

But truth be known, historical facts and figures (i.e. death tolls) are hard to come by, so it would be but guesswork on our part.

That being said, one cannot fail to mention such intimidating devices as **The Staff of Moses**. In Exodus 4, the Lord tells the great prophet of Israel that he will empower Moses with an extraordinary magical staff so that the uninitiated will know that God is omnipotent and should be worshiped above all others. Saith the Lord: *"What is that in your hand?" He said, "A staff." And he said, "Throw it on the ground." So he threw it on the ground, and it became a serpent, and Moses ran from it. But the LORD said to Moses, "Put out your hand and catch it by the tail"—so he put out his hand and caught it, and it became a staff in his hand—"that they may believe that the LORD, the God of their fathers, the God of Abraham, the God of Isaac, and the God of Jacob, has appeared to you." **Exodus 4:2-5 ESV**

< The Ring of Solomon is known in the traditions of Judaism, Christianity and Islam. It is without a doubt the most powerful ring in all of human history. This magic ring variously gave Solomon the power to command demons, the jinn, or to speak with animals. Owing to the proverbial Wisdom of Solomon, his signet ring, or its supposed design, came to be seen as an amulet or talisman, or as a magical symbol or character, in medieval and Renaissance-era magic, occultism and alchemy. According to the Talmud, *Solomon's ring* was engraved with the shem ha-meforesh—the Ineffable

THE ARK OF THE COVENANT AND OTHER SECRET WEAPONS OF THE ANCIENTS

Name of GOD.

The ring is said to have existed as recently as two hundred years ago, when it came into the hands of a private collector. It would be worth tens of millions of dollars if found today

And last, but not least, we need to acknowledge **The Spear of Longinus**, which is sometimes also known as the Spear of Destiny. It is the spear that pierced the side of Christ as he hung on the cross. The Roman soldier Longinus was commanded to lance the Son of God in the side and to penetrate his flesh as deeply as possible in order to make certain that he was indeed dead. The Spear has been thought to possess supernatural traits and is a most powerful weapon that will make

THE ARK OF THE COVENANT AND OTHER SECRET WEAPONS OF THE ANCIENTS

the person or country who wields it victorious in all engagements and military struggles. Constantine and Hitler both wished to own Longinus' Spear because they believed it would enable them to rule the world unchallenged. History did not show favor to either would-be conqueror.

Maria D' Andrea says our past is replete with tales of despicable weapons that have influenced the course of history as well as unseated many a ruler, for better or worse.

"So remember that tales of mythology may have more of a basis in reality than modern man has been willing to acknowledge. We didn't have aircraft to ferry us around yet there are many tales about the 'weapons of the sky,' either helping or destroying. The God who flew on clouds could be helpful, jealous, vengeful or loving, all depending upon his disposition at the time. Many of these supernatural tools they wielded or gave to us were really neutral. It was the practitioner who interpreted their use as positive or negative. So next time someone says something struck them 'from out of the blue,' or that someone was 'right on target' with a remark, be aware of where these expressions were derived."

Indeed, there is plenty of evidence that the ancient gods were NOT figments of the imagination, and, furthermore, that some of the most powerful weapons of all time might have originated in higher realms and could be coming back to haunt the world today!

THE ARK OF THE COVENANT AND OTHER SECRET WEAPONS OF THE ANCIENTS

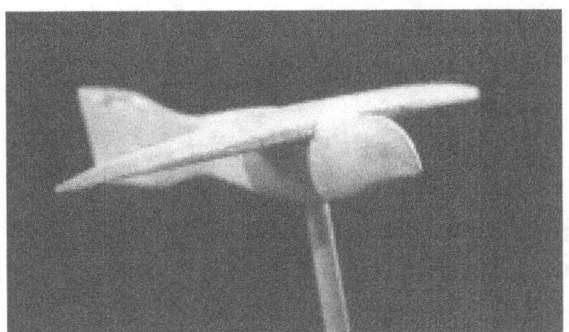

ANCIENT SPACEPORTS AND THE MUSIC OF THE SPHERES

By Tim R. Swartz

The possibility that some ancient civilization may have actually achieved space travel is intriguing, yet not taken very seriously by mainstream scientists. Ancient myths and legends often speak of the gods, or even normal people, flying through the atmosphere and even into space inside of technologically advanced craft. However, despite the proliferation of ancient writings describing such adventures, there has been little physical evidence to lend credence to these stories.

There have been a few artifacts discovered that somewhat resemble modern aircraft. One winged object was found in 1898 in a tomb at Saqquara, Egypt, and was later dated as having been created near 200 BCE. As airplanes were unknown in the days when it was found, it was thrown into a box marked "wooden bird model" and then stored in the basement of the Cairo museum.

It was rediscovered by Dr. Khalil Messiha, who studied models made by ancients. The artifact is made of wood and has a length of 5.6 inches and a wingspan of 7.2 inches. A separate slotted piece fits onto the tail precisely like the back tail wing on a modern plane. Made of very light sycamore, the craft weighs 0.5 oz. and a full-scale version could have flown carrying heavy loads, but at low speeds, between 45 and 65 miles per hour. What is not known, however, is what the power source was. The model makes a perfect glider as it is. Even though over

THE ARK OF THE COVENANT AND OTHER
SECRET WEAPONS OF THE ANCIENTS

2,000 years old, it will soar a considerable distance with only a slight jerk of the hand. Fully restored balsa replicas travel even farther.

Dr. Messiha notes that the ancient Egyptians often built scale models of everything familiar in their daily lives and placed them in their tombs, temples, ships, chariots, servants, animals and so forth. Now that we have found a model plane, Messiha wonders if perhaps somewhere under the desert sands there may yet be unearthed the remains of life-sized gliders.

In north central Colombia hundreds of tiny pieces of gold jewelry were unearthed near the Magdalena River. These golden pendants are shaped like animals, and only a few inches in size. Approximately a dozen of these pieces resemble modern airplanes, yet they are believed to be from the Tolima culture crafted between 500 and 800 BCE.

Archaeologists say the trinkets are supposed to represent stylized versions of birds and insects, even though the wings are attached underneath the body and as far as it is known, no bird, or insect, has upright tail fins. In 1996, a German by the name of Peter Belting created a scale model of one of the pendants to experiment with its flight capabilities. A propeller was added to the nose of the plane and the wings were equipped with flaps and rolls. Early test flights were a success. The plane had a stable flight path and was able to make accurate landings.

So here are two examples of what may have been ancient aircraft, or at least models representing these aircraft. As far as is currently known, no actual ancient airplanes or spaceships have ever been dug out of the ground and hauled off to a museum. However, there are some interesting locations around the planet that may have served as airports, or even spaceports. Whatever the case, the remaining physical evidence found at these sites shows what appears to be an advanced technology far ahead of what is believed to have existed at the time.

THE ARK OF THE COVENANT AND OTHER SECRET WEAPONS OF THE ANCIENTS

The Kutch Figure

A giant figure that resembles the Roman numeral VI composed of wide trenches was discovered near the Havda village in the Kutch district of the western Indian state of Gujarat. Each arm of this feature is a trench that is about three yards wide, six feet deep and more than 200 yards long. Ancient legends in the area say that this area served as a port for travelers from the stars.

Archeologists suggest that the area might have been used as a spaceport by the Harappan civilization, which had one of the most fascinating yet mysterious cultures in the ancient world. Located along the Indus River in modern-day Pakistan, this civilization was named after the city of Harappa and is famous for its incredible knowledge of astronomy. Harappan priest-astronomers closely followed the planetary movements composing a star-calendar that was later adopted by the Aryans.

Excavations in India had previously shown that the ancient settlers suddenly abandoned and re-inhabited their fortified city in the Kutch reigion several times for reasons yet unknown.

China's Ancient Spaceport

In the depths of the Qaidam Basin, Qinghai Province of northwest China at the foot of Mount Baigong, is a mysterious site that locals say is the remains of a spaceport used by the original inhabitants of the region. It should be immediately noted that the word "Baigong" means "Hill" in the local dialect.

What makes this place so unusual are the metal pipes found throughout the area. The pipes were first discovered by a group of U.S. scientists searching for dinosaur fossils. The pipes were reported to the local authorities in Delingha. A story about the discovery was published in June, 2002, by the Henan Great River News. The local government has promoted the pipe-like features as a tourist attraction with

THE ARK OF THE COVENANT AND OTHER SECRET WEAPONS OF THE ANCIENTS

road signs and tourist guides.

The rusty tubes, ranging from needle-size to 16 inches in diameter, reach from deep inside the mountain to a saltwater lake 260 feet away. Many of the hollow pipes are uniform in size and seem to be placed purposefully. The ancient objects are embedded deep enough into the mountain wall and floor to preclude modern human handling.

The pipes, according to tests carried out at a local smeltery, are made chiefly of iron, but with an unusual thirty percent silicon dioxide in their matrix. The silicon dioxide and calcium oxide are products of long interaction between the iron and surrounding sandstone, showing the ancient age of the pipes. Liu Shaolin, the engineer who did the analysis, told the Xinhua news agency, "This result has made the site even more mysterious." Dating done by the Beijing Institute of Geology determined these iron pipes were smelted about 150,000 years ago. The dating was done using thermo-luminescence, a technique that determines how long ago crystalline mineral was exposed to sunlight or heated. Humans are only thought to have inhabited the region for the past 30,000 years. Even within the known history of the area, the only humans to inhabit the region were nomads whose lifestyle would not leave any such structures behind.

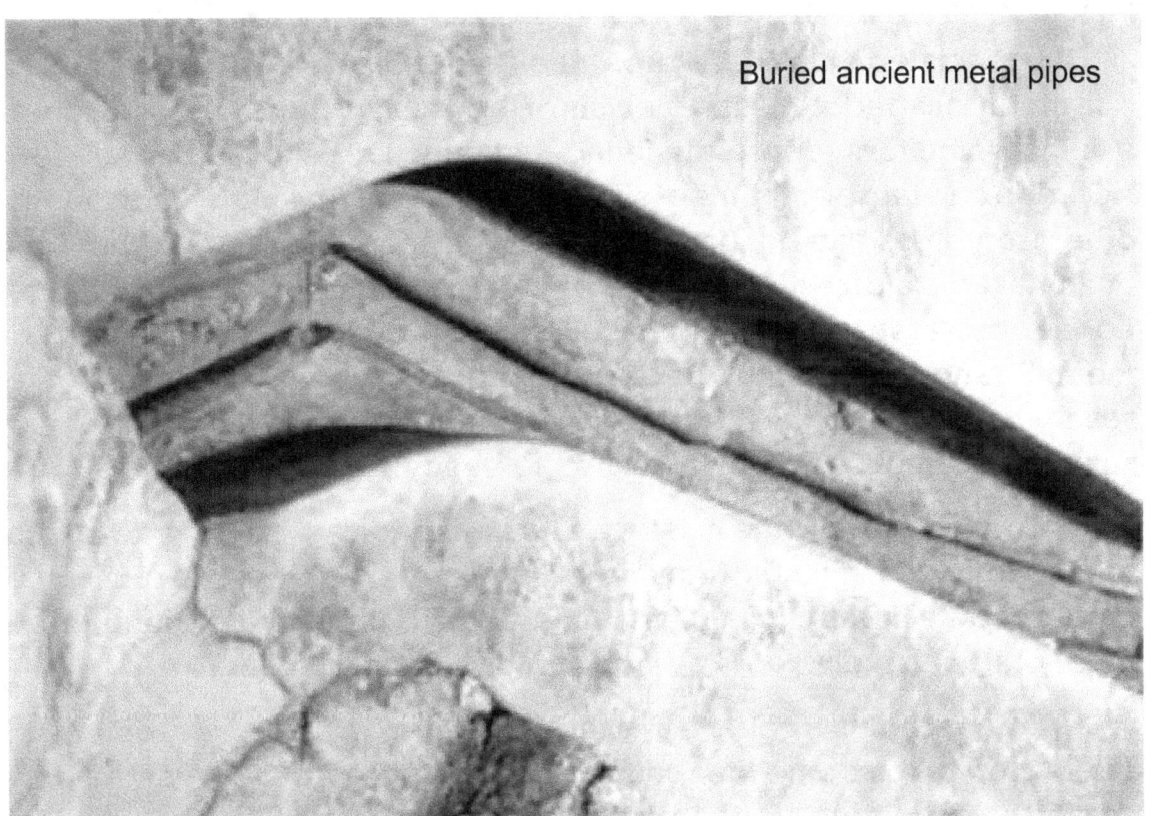

Buried ancient metal pipes

The area is dominated by twin lakes dubbed as the "Lover Lakes," one with fresh water and the other with salty water. The relics are located on the south bank of the salty lake named Toson. Next to the lake lie three caves, the largest and most accessible some 27 feet high by twenty feet deep. Inside, spanning from the roof to the back end of the cave runs a pipe 15 inches in diameter. Another pipe roughly the same size runs into the earth from the floor, with just the top protruding.

THE ARK OF THE COVENANT AND OTHER SECRET WEAPONS OF THE ANCIENTS

Additional Baigong Pipes were found onshore and within Toson Lake. On the beach, flat-lying, hollow, pipe-like features are found. These reddish-brown pipe-like features range in diameter from 0.8 to 1.8 inches and have an east-west orientation. Another group of pipe-like features, presumably vertical, either protrude from or lie just below the surface of the lake.

Associated with these pipe-like features are "rusty scraps" and "strangely shaped stones." Analysis of the "rusty scraps" by Liu Shaolin at a local smelters reportedly found that they consist of 30 percent ferric oxide and large amounts of silicon dioxide and calcium oxide. Many other iron pipes can be found scattered on sands and rocks. They run in an east-west direction and are of various strange shapes. The thinnest is like a toothpick, but not blocked inside after years of sand movement. Stranger still is that there are also some pipes in the lake, some reaching above the water surface and some buried below, with similar shapes and thickness with those on the beach.

To further add to the mystery, Zheng Jiandong, a geology research fellow from the China Earthquake Administration, told state-run newspaper People's Daily in 2007 that some of the pipes were found to be highly radioactive.

Some scientists believe that the pipes are fossilized tree root casts. The rusted tubes being the result of tree roots that underwent the processes of pedogenesis (the process that forms soils) and diagenesis (transformation of soil into rock). However, if this is the case, it would be thought that more "pipes" would be found all over the region. Unfortunately for the more conventional theory, this is not the case. The pipes are only found in the Mt. Baigong area.

UFO researchers, especially in China, have attributed the pipes to ancient extraterrestrial visitors. But, local legends state that there was once a civilization that existed thousands of years before recorded

THE ARK OF THE COVENANT AND OTHER SECRET WEAPONS OF THE ANCIENTS

history that was so technologically advanced as to have achieved space flight. The Mount Baigong region was one of many places around the planet that this now extinct civilization used to launch their space ships out into the far reaches of the galaxy.

The mythologies of the Baigong area also state that the now-vanished rulers of the world used music to help construct their great cities and monuments. This is an interesting possibility, as there are other legends scattered across the globe that state almost exactly the same thing – that music, or sound, was important in ancient ceremonies and structures.

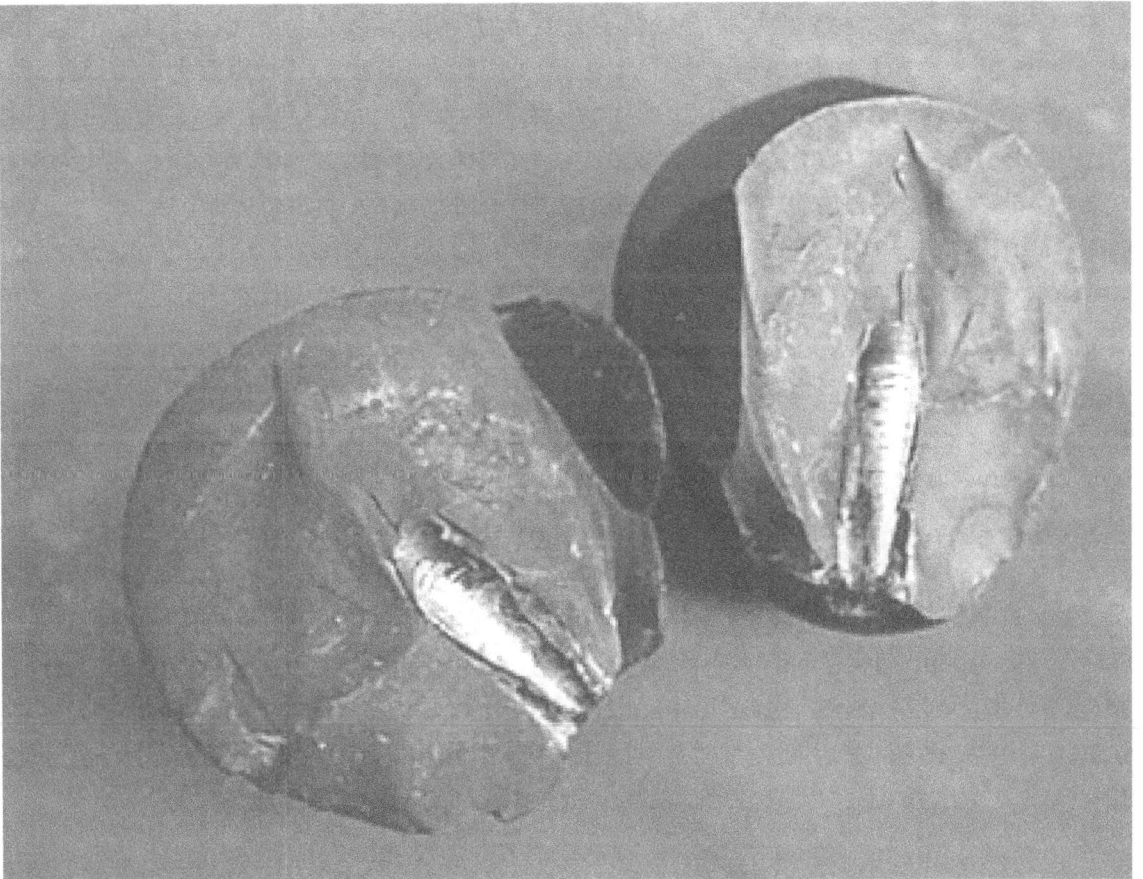

When cut, this stone was found to have a shaped metal object embedded inside.

THE ARK OF THE COVENANT AND OTHER SECRET WEAPONS OF THE ANCIENTS

The Walls of Jericho Came Tumbling Down

Keeping us on track, the mystical and magical Maria D' Andrea, a psychic and author, reminds us that the tools of power utilized by the wizards of olden days came in various forms. "The heavens would open and the divine power would strike them. Maybe it was unseen, or perhaps it was a beam from an extraterrestrial space ship sent from the gods who resided light years away. This energy that struck them cut across all barriers of time and space. If the aim of the gods is true, nothing can prevent them from sharing their powers with mortal collaborators.

"Symbols and colors, varying degrees of hot and cold, as well as the use of sound, added to the vitality and potency of the transmissions between humans and their source of 'inspiration.' We are told in the Bible that the walls of Jericho came tumbling down after the Israelite army marched around the city blowing their trumpets. There are some that think that sound and frequency played an important role in ancient cultures, including in the building of the pyramids of Egypt."

Recent investigations into Paleolithic cave-art have revealed an association between areas which produce a strong resonance and the location of the art. This finding demonstrates that the properties of sound were being recognized, explored, appreciated and recorded over 30,000 years ago.

"Scientists analyze 3,000 year old Conch Shell"

Archaeologists unearthed 20 complete Strombus galeatus marine shell trumpets in 2001 at Chavín de Huántar, an ancient ceremonial center in the Andes. Polished, painted and etched with symbols, the shells had well-formed mouthpieces and distinct V-shaped cuts.

If the shells were played inside the stone chamber in which they were found, the drone would have sounded like it was coming from several different directions at once. In the dimly lit religious centre, it

THE ARK OF THE COVENANT AND OTHER SECRET WEAPONS OF THE ANCIENTS

would have created a sense of confusion.

- Discovery News, 2010.

A story was told by the local Aymara Indians to a Spanish traveler who visited Tiahuanaco shortly after the conquest. The story spoke of the city's original foundation in the age of Chamac Pacha, or First Creation, long before the coming of the Incas. Its earliest inhabitants, they said, possessed supernatural powers with which they were miraculously able to lift stones off the ground. The stones "were carried (from the mountain quarries) through the air to the sound of a trumpet."

Mayan legends say that the temple of Uxmal, in Mexico, was built by a race of dwarves, which apparently only had to whistle and "heavy rocks would move into place." It is said that if a person stands at the base of the pyramid-like Temple of the magician and claps their hands the stone structure at the top produces a "chirping sound."

According to classical Greek writers, Thebes, the capital of Boeotia, was founded by Cadmus, a celebrated Phoenician. It was finished off, the story goes, by a son of Jupiter named Amphion, who was able to move large stones to the sound of a lyre or harp, by which manner he was able to construct the walls of Thebes. Appollonius Rhodius, who lived in the third century BC, poetically recalled in Argonautica how Amphion would sing loud and clear on his golden lyre as large rocks followed his footsteps. Traditions surrounding Cadmus clearly indicate that Thebes was founded by Phoenician migrants who must have settled there in the third or second millennium BC.

Phoenicia's oldest known historian, Sanchaniatho, spoke of the god Ouranus or Coelus founding the first city at a place called Byblos. He also said that one of the gods, "Taautus" (the Egyptian Thoth), founded the Egyptian civilization. He also states that Ouranus "devised Baetulia, contriving stones that moved as having life."

In the early 20th century, a Swedish doctor is reputed to have wit-

THE ARK OF THE COVENANT AND OTHER SECRET WEAPONS OF THE ANCIENTS

nessed stone blocks 1.5 meters in length and a meter in height and width being levitated through the air through the process of sound.

Dr. Jarl studied at Oxford. During those times he became friends with a young Tibetan student. A couple of years later – it was 1939 – Dr. Jarl made a journey to Egypt for the English Scientific Society. There he was seen by a messenger of his Tibetan friend and urgently requested to come to Tibet to treat a high Lama.

After Dr. Jarl got the leave, he followed the messenger and arrived, after a long journey by plane and Yak caravans, at the monastery where the old Lama and his friend were now living. Jarl stayed there for some time, and, because of his friendship with the Tibetans, he learned a lot of things that other foreigners had no chance to hear about or observe.

One day his friend took him to a place in the neighborhood of the monastery and showed him a sloping meadow that was surrounded in the northwest by high cliffs. In one of the rock walls, at a height of about 250 meters, was a big hole that looked like the entrance to a cave. In front of this hole there was a platform on which the monks were building a rock wall. The only access to this platform was from the top of the cliff. The monks lowered themselves down with the help of ropes.

In the middle of the meadow, about 250 meters from the cliff, was a polished slab of rock with a bowl-like cavity in the center. The bowl had a diameter of one meter and a depth of 15 centimeters. A block of stone was maneuvered into this cavity by Yak oxen. The block was one meter wide and one and one half meters long. Then 19 musical instruments were set in an arc of 90 degrees at a distance of 63 meters from the stone slab.

The radius of 63 meters was measured out accurately. The musical instruments consisted of 13 drums and 6 trumpets (Ragdons). Eight drums had a cross-section of one meter and a length of one and one half meters. Four drums were medium size, with a cross-section of 0.7 meter and a length of one meter. The only small drum had a cross-section of 0.2 meters and a length of 0.3 meters. All the trumpets were the same size.

They had a length of 3.12 meters and an opening of 0.3 meters. The big drums and all the trumpets were fixed on mounts which could be adjusted with staffs in the direction of the slab of stone. The big drums were made of 1mm thick sheet iron, and had a weight of 150kg. They were built in five sections. All the drums were open at one end, while the other end had a bottom of metal, on which the monks beat with big leather clubs. Behind each instrument was a row of monks.

When the stone was in position, the monk behind the small drum gave a signal to start the concert. The small drum had a very sharp sound and could be heard even with the other instruments making a terrible din. All the monks were singing and chanting a prayer, slowly increasing the tempo of this unbelievable noise. During the first four minutes nothing happened, then, as the speed of the drumming and the noise increased, the big stone block started to rock and sway. Suddenly it took off into the air with an increasing speed in the direction of the platform in front of the cave hole 250 meters high. After three minutes of ascent it landed on the platform.

Continuously they brought new blocks to the meadow, and the monks, using this method, transported five to six blocks per hour on a parabolic flight track approximately 500 meters long and 250 meters high. From time to time a stone split, and the monks moved the split stones away.

Dr. Jarl knew about the hurling of the stones. Tibetan experts like Linaver, Spalding and Huc had spoken about it but they had never seen it. So Dr. Jarl was the first foreigner who had the opportunity to see this remarkable spectacle. Because he had the opinion in the beginning

THE ARK OF THE COVENANT AND OTHER
SECRET WEAPONS OF THE ANCIENTS

that he was the victim of mass-psychosis, he made two films of the incident. The films showed exactly the same things that he had witnessed.

In the past, researchers at Northwestern Polytechnic University in Xi'an, China, used ultrasound fields to successfully levitate globs of the heaviest solid and liquid — iridium and mercury, respectively. The aim of their work is to learn how to manufacture everything from pharmaceuticals to alloys without the aid of containers. At times, compounds are too corrosive for containers to hold or they react with containers in other undesirable ways.

"An interesting question is, 'What will happen if a living animal is put into the acoustic field?' Will it also be stably levitated?" asked researcher Wenjun Xie, a materials physicist at Northwestern Polytechnical University.

Xie and his colleagues employed an ultrasound emitter and reflector that generated a sound pressure field between them. The emitter produced roughly 20-millimeter-wavelength sounds, meaning it could in theory levitate objects half that wavelength or less.

After the investigators got the ultrasound field going, they used tweezers to carefully place animals between the emitter and reflector. The scientists found they could float ants, beetles, spiders, ladybirds, bees, tadpoles and fish up to a little more than a third of an inch long in midair. When they levitated a fish and tadpole, the researchers added water to the ultrasound field every minute via syringe.

The levitated ant tried crawling in the air and struggled to escape by rapidly flexing its legs, although it generally failed because its feet found little purchase in the air. The ladybug tried flying away but also failed when the field was too strong to break away from.

The power of sound has been demonstrated by opera singers who have been known, on occasion, to shatter glass simply by producing the correct sound. This effect was presumably already understood with

THE ARK OF THE COVENANT AND OTHER SECRET WEAPONS OF THE ANCIENTS

the story of the shattering of the walls of Jericho as written in the Old Testament:

"Then the Lord said to Joshua, 'See, I have delivered Jericho into your hands, along with its king and its fighting men. March around the city once with all the armed men. Do this for six days. Have seven priests carry trumpets of rams' horns in front of the ark. On the seventh day, march around the city seven times, with the priests blowing the trumpets. When you hear them sound a long blast on the trumpets, have the whole army give a loud shout; then the wall of the city will collapse and the army will go up, everyone straight in.'" Joshua 6:2-5

Jericho is the name of an ancient city situated close to a lake in Palestine. The name is well known from the Biblical story where God commands Joshua to destroy the city because of its inhabitants' disobedience to God, as the above abstract mentions; but the story of the city goes back to about 8000 BCE when it was occupied during the Natufian period, making the structures in it the oldest manmade structures on Earth.

The archaeological evidence has verified that the Biblical story is accurate. Excavations show that Jericho was destroyed in approximately 1400 BCE, and that a portion of the city was burned completely.

The battle of Jericho is an amazing tale, with the description of the Ark of the Covenant and the trumpets used as a weapon under the command of Joshua and the orders of God himself. It wasn't just a simple fight; these weapons were so powerful that they were capable of completely destroying an entire city in seven days. With the exception of a prostitute — who was thought to have betrayed her fellow citizens — and her family, every single living being died. After that the city was cursed by Joshua to never be built again; however the city was rebuilt many times after that event.

Jericho was a city heavily fortified and stocked with enough food

THE ARK OF THE COVENANT AND OTHER SECRET WEAPONS OF THE ANCIENTS

and water to last for months. It would have taken many months — even years — to destroy such a city, and yet Joshua did it, according to the Bible, in seven days. Ancient astronaut theorists have argued that some kind of superior weaponry provided by an external, perhaps even "alien," interfering force was used in the destruction of Jericho. This is a mystery still unresolved.

Nikola Tesla's Speculations on the Ark of the Covenant

For centuries, the Ark was viewed as a mystical object from God, beyond the knowledge of man. However, that changed on September 9, 1915, when the famous scientist Nikola Tesla published an article entitled "The Wonder World to be Created by Electricity." In it, he made the following astounding claim:

"Moses was undoubtedly a practical and skillful electrician far in advance of his time. The Bible describes precisely and minutely arrangements constituting a machine in which electricity was generated by friction of air against silk curtains and stored in a box constructed like a condenser. It is very plausible to assume that the sons of Aaron were killed by a high tension discharge."

If we take Tesla's speculation a step further by assuming that the Ark of the Covenant was capable of generating great power, perhaps this power was used to produce sound powerful enough to bring down the walls of Jericho – and even kill.

Sound is a waveform, with low infrasonic frequencies having a long wave length (measured in tens of meters), and with high ultrasonic frequencies having a short wave length (measured in millimeters). The frequencies associated with ultrasound are most familiar from their utilization by the medical profession, chiefly for diagnostic imaging.

While the ears are designed to detect a limited range of frequencies – the human auditory range is between 20Hz and 20,000Hz (1Hz = 1

THE ARK OF THE COVENANT AND OTHER SECRET WEAPONS OF THE ANCIENTS

cycle per second) – different frequencies can affect the whole body and, at volume, can be felt in almost any part of the body. Even with industrial ear protectors, sound waves are able to enter the head via the nose and mouth which are, in turn, linked to the ears by the structure of the skull. Sounds that are higher in frequency than 20,000Hz – ultrasound – are inaudible to humans, while sounds lower than 20Hz – infrasound – are inaudible but can, on occasion, be felt resonating within the body itself. Exposure of unprotected ears to infrasound can also cause an increase in pressure within the middle ear, disturbing the sense of balance.

The potential of infrasound to affect the human body has long been apparent; as anybody who has leaned against the PA at a rave will tell you, even audible sub-bass frequencies at the correct volume can churn your stomach. The theory behind infrasound weapons tends to focus on the idea that certain frequencies can be used as both a weapon and as a method of crowd control.

According to the Working Paper on Infrasound Weapons produced by Hungary for the United Nations in 1978, the frequency that is thought to be most dangerous to humans is between 7 and 8Hz. This is the resonant frequency of flesh and, theoretically, it can rupture internal organs if loud enough.

It appears that modern science is finally starting to catch up to the secrets that now nearly forgotten ancient civilizations used to heal, build, travel to the stars, and ultimately destroy themselves. Will history repeat itself? Will our civilization succumb to the temptations that seduced our predecessors...allowing ourselves to be overcome by greed and the lust for power and ultimately unleashing the music of the spheres to silence our voices forever?

Will those who next walk upon this planet discover the broken remains of our world and wonder who we were and how we managed to take our great knowledge and obliterate ourselves almost completely?

We are left to wonder if this is a cycle that we are all trapped within. Like prehistoric insects frozen forever within drops of amber. Doomed to repeat the mistakes of those who came before, arising from the dust and sending ourselves back, again and again for eternity.

THE ARK OF THE COVENANT AND OTHER SECRET WEAPONS OF THE ANCIENTS

THE ARK OF THE COVENANT AND OTHER SECRET WEAPONS OF THE ANCIENTS

**RECOMMENDED READING
BOOKS BY
TIM R. SWARTZ**

Time Travel: Fact Not Fiction

Secret Lost Diary of Richard Byrd and the Phantom of the Poles

Lost Journals of Nikola Tesla

Strange and Unexplainable Deaths

Mind Stalkers Out of the Darkness

Men of Mystery

World of Sherlock Holmes

Reality of the Inner Earth

Available from Amazon.com

ConspiracyJournal.com

**RECOMMENDED READING
BOOKS BY
BRAD STEIGER**

Mysteries of Time and Space

Real Ghosts Restless Spirits

Real Aliens, Space Beings and Creatures From Other Worlds

Rainbow Conspiracies

Real Encounters, Different Dimensions and Other Worldly Beings

Conspiracies and Secret Societies

The Other

Revelations The Divine Fire

Over 200 Titles

Available from Amazon.com

BradAndSherry.com

THE ARK OF THE COVENANT AND OTHER SECRET WEAPONS OF THE ANCIENTS

Timothy Green Beckley

Sean Casteel

Olav Phillips

Brad and Sherry Steiger

Tim R. Swartz

THE ARK OF THE COVENANT AND OTHER
SECRET WEAPONS OF THE ANCIENTS

www.ingramcontent.com/pod-product-compliance
Lightning Source LLC
Chambersburg PA
CBHW081212280526
45787CB00006B/2388